The Journey With God

The Journey With God

Living With Purpose and Joy

Creath Davis

Person to Person BOOKS

BAKER BOOK HOUSE
Grand Rapids, Michigan 49516

©1971, 1981 by Creath Davis
Revised edition 1988

Originally published by:
Zondervan Publishing House
Beyond This God Cannot Go
Grand Rapids, Michigan

Baker Book House
ISBN 0-8010-2982-1

Person to Person Books
ISBN 0-933973-03-9

All rights reserved. No portion of this book may be used or reproduced in any form without written permission of the publisher except in the case of brief quotations within critical articles and reviews.

Printed in the United States of America

To my wife
VERDELL
and children
David, Shawna and Stephen
who have taught me the meaning of love

CONTENTS

Foreword ix

Preface xi

1. How to Begin the Journey with God 1
2. Keeping Up the Appearances.................. 11
3. What About My Past? 21
4. What About My Future? 31
5. The Need for Self-Acceptance 41
6. God's Magnificent Obsession 53
7. Isolation Is Insanity 65
8. For Better or For Worse 81
9. What About My Vocation? 97
10. Not for My Sake Alone 109
11. Finding an Adequate Motivation for the Journey 121

Beyond This God Cannot Go —
  A Poem by Verdell Davis..................... 131

Epilogue: They Have Found the Plane 133

Creath Davis: A Tribute 139

Acknowledgments 140

Notes 143

FOREWORD

It was my privilege to share in Creath's life and ministry for more than twenty-seven years. Creath blessed my life far beyond what I ever would have dreamed or asked. I sat at his feet, as did many, many others, and learned from him that to choose to walk with God is to embark on a journey with the living Christ in meeting the needs of a lost and hurting world.

In this his first book Creath wrote, "When God gets hold of someone, it is not for his sake alone. It is through this one life that He purposes to touch others in a redemptive way." He calls us to ask God to give us a love for Him and His purpose that runs deeper than the love of our own life. He dares us to taste a greatness that this world knows nothing of.

It is my prayer that each of us who read this book will open our hearts and lives to the God who created us and allow Him to make of us the kind of people that can change that part of the world we touch.

Let us never lose the awe and wonder of being caught up with the God of the Universe in His eternal plan.

MRS. CREATH DAVIS
May 1988

PREFACE

This book is an expression of my own search and struggle as one man seeking to find himself in the midst of the confusion and revolution of the twentieth century. It is a composite of the experiences and concepts which have shaped my life to this point. As it has turned out this book could actually be identified as my understanding of what Christianity really is and how Jesus Christ can make an exciting difference in every area of one's life. This is the culmination of a search which began in my boyhood.

When I was a young boy I'd often go out at night and stand on our cellar door and look at the vastness above and ask, "Why am I here? Is there really a God out there? If He's out there, does He know that I'm down here?"

At that time in my life I had contact with only one person who had a significant faith—my grandmother. She was a special person to me. She had taught school, eleven grades in one room, but when I knew her she was crippled and spent most of her time in a wheel chair. I sat for hours in her lap or beside her chair and listened wide-eyed to the things she would tell me. In retrospect, I think it was her love for me and her faith in a God who cared for everyone that sent me in search of this God she seemed to know.

I concluded that there must be a reason for everyone to be alive, even me. I reasoned I could have just as easily not been born as to have been born, so there must be a purpose for my being alive. This left me with the one big question, "What is that purpose?" *To find the reason for my being alive became my quest,* and it continues to be to this very moment. From what others have shared with me, I can see that this is our quest—the quest of the whole human race. It may be expressed in many different ways, but it is just as real as life itself.

My journey has led me from serving as a pastor for nine years to being the Director of both an adult retreat center, Kaleo Lodge, and a counseling center for the past sixteen years. This has given me the incredible opportunity to monitor the practical results of men and women responding to the gospel in almost every conceivable situation. I have become increasingly more convinced that Frances Shaeffer's term "true truth" is most appropriate when speaking of God's Good News as we have it in the scriptures.

I invite you to explore with me this Good News.

CHAPTER 1

HOW TO BEGIN THE JOURNEY WITH GOD

Except a man be born again . . .

I began my Christian pilgrimage over twenty-five years ago in a layman's home. I had little knowledge of the Christian message, but my friend had something I wanted—an exciting relationship with Jesus Christ! He shared with me very simply, from the Scriptures and from his own experience, how he had invited Jesus Christ to come into his life. Out of my own sense of need and search, I committed my life to Christ. In his living room I prayed, "Oh, Lord, I'm in a mess. I need You to change my life. I invite You to come in and do in me what needs to be done." To my utter amazement He did come in, and I had a deep sense of forgiveness and acceptance. This was the beginning for me. Life looked different, and it still does.

We cannot understand ourselves or explain ourselves in a single event. A snapshot is not adequate. A moving picture is needed if we are to really understand a person.

My wife has two pictures of me, one placed in the bedroom and one in the living room. In one picture I have on a suit and in the other I am sitting on the peak of a mountain in Switzerland. Out of my masculine pride I jokingly said to her, "In one picture you see what I look like but in the other you see what I am like; or at least what I would like for you to think I'm like." Yet she knows that these two pictures do not begin to capture the real me. She knows me, because she shares life with me. This is not to minimize any experience or event of life, but to say that even the most significant event is only a part of me. To understand ourselves we must see ourselves in movement, with every single event making its impact and with our response to those events actually shaping our destiny.

Life is a journey, packed full of a variety of experiences, some of which bring about radical changes within us. This means life is open-ended, with the potential of being as empty or as full as we allow it to be. It does not matter what we have or have not been. Life for us can be different!

There is one experience that can change life from just being movement, and cause it to become movement with purpose and destiny. That experience involves our relationship to the God who made us. There is a restlessness in all of us that only God can satisfy. But it is a strange phenomenon that we try to satisfy that restlessness with everything except God and seem to turn God-ward only as a last resort.

This is the heart of every person's problem—rebellion. To understand the nature of our rebellion we need some understanding of essential man and existential man. Essential man is man as he was intended to be. This is man as described in Psalm 8, man made "a little lower than God";[1] or as the writer of Genesis says, "God created man in His own image."[2] This means that physically we are akin to the rest of creation, but spiritually we are akin to God Himself, with the capacity and responsibility of responding to God. We are not gods, but creatures of God, dependent upon God for our very existence. Man was crowned with glory and honor as the climax of God's creation. He possessed a dignity of his own and the ability to achieve far beyond his wildest imagination. Man was to have dominion over the works of God's hands, and the arena in which he was to express himself was the cosmic universe. Imagine, a universe as man's backyard laboratory! This creature of God was given such potential that the only adequate center for his life was God. Anything less than God was too small for releasing the potential within him.

When we look at man as he actually is we see a fallen creature. Humans have made great advances in many areas, it is true. The image of God has been marred, but not destroyed. To see man progressing from the stone age to the atomic age is to witness the incredible. To read of the civilizing effect that some nations in history have had on the rest of the world is phenomenal. The advances in our own century in medicine and psychology are other milestones in man's achievements. Yet for all of his achievements, man remains a mystery to himself. He finds himself a tension-filled unity with infinite potential, both divine and demonic. To his dismay, the demonic is continually apparent. Mixed with the history of human achievements is the history of wars, greed and lust.

There is a spiritual and moral insanity which man, alone, cannot overcome. Ever since Adam in the Garden of Eden rebelled against God, every person, except one, has repeated that rebellion. With our stress on rugged individualism in the West, it is hard for us to understand how one man's sin could so affect the whole human race. There seems to be a subterranean unity of the human race, making it possible for one person deeply to affect another without losing his own uniqueness. This reality makes possible meaningful relationships, but it also means that the good I do and the evil I do go far beyond myself. It is poured into the heritage of all people in some fashion.

Through Adam man has been bent in the direction of rebellion, but he is not responsible for Adam's sin. What makes us responsible is the crystallizing of our own rebellion against God. Much of this rebellion exists below the conscious level, but some of it is deliberately choosing our own way over the way of love—which is the way of God. The symptoms of this rebellion may take many shapes, from vulgar, overt acts to more subtle, sophisticated acts. One man may murder, steal or commit adultery, while another may criticize, exploit or meet people by presenting only a facade, never allowing his real self to be known. These are but symptoms of a deeper, inner disease which is pouring its poison into the total personality, keeping that person from thinking right, feeling right, acting right, or being right. It is the nature of this inner disease (which pushes us in the direction of rebellion) that we need to understand—not just the symptoms.

Facing the implications of the biblical teachings concerning the nature of this inner distortion is like reading my own mail. This rebellion is not something we thought about, but it is something we acted out. It begins somewhere along the way, when we try to put self in that God-sized vacuum within. We become our own god, going our own way, with the attitude that where we stand is the center of the world and nothing is important except what affects us personally. In confronting myself with this indictment, I see how I can be more concerned over one good toothache (if it is mine) than over a war in another country. No longer is God important except as He can be brought into my orbit to be used and manipulated for selfish reasons.

We have declared our independence in the face of all that declares our dependence. All of our experience tells us we are dependent. We were not born of ourselves. We cannot sustain ourselves. We are dependent upon other people, to a large degree, for the development of our own personalities and for a meaningful place in life. Yet our attitude can become one of self-sufficiency, or one of a sick kind of dependence upon others which demands first place in their attention. We act as did the people in Judges 17:6, ". . . but every man did that which was right in his own eyes." We live a lie! While desperately needing someone greater than ourselves to help us, we act as if we had the world by the tail. What madness! To deny this kind of self-centeredness is to deny the most obvious truth about ourselves. But deny it we do. It becomes too raw a reality to acknowledge that we have asked God to abandon His place to us. In comes subtle self-deceit, a kind of blindness that deliberately closes its eyes to the truth in order to maintain its position.

Once this kingdom of self is established, pride enters; then a man will not tolerate anyone or anything who threatens to overshadow him—even God. Unless this attitude is faced with repentance, it becomes so vicious that it will produce people who are God-murderers at heart. This is the reason the Scripture declares us to be guilty of the death of Christ. We were not at the cross personally, but the same inner distortion that caused those men in that day to carry out the crucifixion is in us. And, unless that distortion is remedied, something in us would rise to destroy that same God if He drew near with His demanding love today.

With this ugly distortion comes the progressive deterioration of character. All of the great God-given capacities, which were meant to be turned outward to increase life, are turned inward for selfish gratification, and life is impoverished. Love and sex are good examples of these. They offer mankind the possibility of the most intimate relationship and unity. Yet, with love and sex becoming an expression of self-centeredness, frustration and unnaturalness enter. The result is exploitation of the other person and perversion of the sex drive.

The evil men do is tragic, but even more tragic is the good they miss. It is tragic to use sex for selfish gratification, but it is more grievous to miss the purpose and quality of sex within marriage. Sex is one of the strongest drives within human personality. In this experience God offers an avenue for two people who love each other and who have cast their lives together in marriage to achieve a oneness symbolic of the oneness that abides in the Godhead. Once this expression of shared life is achieved, the stage is set for bringing children into the world and giving them a fair chance. Apart from God this kind of relationship can never be completely achieved.

Perhaps the most devastating blow that sin brings is a sense of utter aloneness. Man has cut himself off from God, from his fellows, and he is inwardly divided against himself. To be lost to the power of love and to be locked inside one's self is the greatest "lostness" of all. Man is left with the feeling that he is alone—against the whole world. It is this inner isolation that will finally break him.

Some may feel that my indictment against mankind is too strong. There is a practical test that can be made, if a person really wants to know the truth about himself. Perhaps this truth can best be illustrated by relating a personal experience. I had a friend who, like many of us, was a real mixed-up fellow. He and his wife couldn't get along. In a fight he literally stomped his grown son. In fact, you would have to think a long time to find any reason to compliment him. As we talked one day, he turned the conversation toward religion. He said to me in all sincerity, "Creath, you know, the Lord and I have always been on pretty good terms." I was shocked. As far as anyone knew Bill never gave even a passing thought to God. Furthemore, I knew he didn't feel that he had to impress me as a minister. I knew too much about him, for I had been his neighbor and friend for several years. But Bill was dead serious. He didn't seem to have any deep pangs about the emptiness in his own life or the misery he was creating for those closest to him. Perhaps he was aware underneath, but he was obviously lying to himself, not to me.

About that time I was in the midst of some growing pains of my own, sensing for myself what spiritual bankruptcy is—something within that resists God. I shared this realization with Bill, but he did not understand, so I gave him a Scripture that was beginning to have real meaning for me. It was John 16:7-11, where the Lord is preparing His disciples for His own death and is promising them the Holy Spirit as a Helper: "It is for your good that I am going away. Unless I go away, the Counselor will not come to you; but if I go, I will send him to you. When he comes, he will prove the world wrong about sin and righteousness and judgment: about sin, because men do not believe in me; about righteousness, because I am going to the Father, where you can see me no longer; and about judgment, because the prince of this world now stands condemned." (NIV) The Lord said that the Holy Spirit would convict the world of sin because men did not believe in Him. The way a man responds to Jesus of Nazareth indicates the way he is responding to God, because Jesus of Nazareth is God.

I asked Bill how he felt about Jesus Christ—had he ever been able to find anything wrong with Him? He answered, "Oh, no. I believe He's God!"

Do you think He really cares about you?" I asked.

"Oh, I believe that He does care about me, and everyone else for that matter."

"Do you think He can be trusted? I asked, still skeptical.

"I believe He is God and that He can be trusted," he assured me.

"Bill, do you believe that He wants to do something really great in your life? Give you a new kind of life that can be exciting and full?"

"Yes, I suppose so."

"Do you believe He can really change your life?"

"Sure, I think He can," he replied.

(In spite of his declaration of faith, I still felt that Bill didn't really understand what he was saying, so I decided to press the issue.)

"Bill, you and I have talked about this before, but since you feel that He could really give you a new kind of life, more meaningful than life as you know it now, would you commit yourself to Christ for Him to do His work in you right now?"

Very quickly he responded, "Not yet."

I asked, "Why not?"

He answered, "I just couldn't now."

(The whole tenor of the conversation had changed. From his own mouth he had indicated that there was no reason for him to refuse to commit his life to Jesus Christ.)

"Bill, now you know what our real problem is. If nothing was wrong with us on the inside, when God drew near in love and offered to give us life that is really meaningful and to get inside our problems and enable us to solve them, well, we wouldn't have to be asked twice. We'd jump in with both feet at that kind of invitation from the Living God. But the truth is, none of us responds like that. There is something within all of us that is blind and unreasonable—that resists God without a cause. The Lord has to pursue us, and we stubbornly flee Him. It seems that we only turn to Him out of desperation."

The conversation continued, but the climate was different. For the first time in my experience with him, Bill was deeply convicted and allowed me to share in his inner struggle.

When men see Christ as He is, and face the reality of His love and deliberately resist that love, then they know what sin is. They have experienced it!

Our plight is so desperate that no humanism can bridge the gap. No psychology can heal the brokenness. Only the intervention of God can redeem us.

The universal message of the Christian faith is that God has acted in history on our behalf. God's action was radical, because our problem is radical. God's action is seen clearly in Christ, in all that He was and all that He did. However, it is the cross that is the focal point of the Gospel. It is the cross of Christ that shows us the ugliness of sin and the unbelievable capacity of love. Perfect love in one Man was met with blind hate, which resulted in crucifixion—the depth of man's perversion acted out for all to witness.

Yet, God's love could not be focused more clearly than in His willingness to endure even a cross on our behalf. From that cross God is shouting to His world, "I love you!" This is not weak, indulgent love, but love with strength. Our response, or lack of response, to that limitless love will either free us or shut us up to ourselves forever. No one can be the same after facing God in His agonizing love.

The Scriptures declare, "God was in Christ, reconciling the world unto himself." This reconciliation means the possibility of a new dimension in relationships because of the decisive act of God which removes the hostility and estrangement. The door has been opened not only for us to find peace with God, but with ourselves and our fellows. The door has been opened so wide that the final invitation in the last book of the New Testament is ". . . whosoever will, let him take the water of life freely."[4]

God has acted, but we must respond to that action. We

each must respond for ourselves. This is the real place of beginning for each of us.

How do I find and respond to this God who has acted? This is the question that must be answered. He cannot be known through the intellect, or through philosophy, or even through theology. He cannot be researched like objective scientific data. God is a Person, and He must be known as a Person—through an intimate, personal relationship. The religious leaders of Jesus' day thought they could find God in religious activities. Jesus said to them, "You study the scriptures because you think that in them you will find eternal life. And they themselves speak about me."[5] The Scriptures themselves are written to lead men to nothing less than a personal encounter with God.

What are the conditions for this confrontation with God? The first condition is a sense of need. No one is ready for a Savior who does not know he needs to be saved. To people in His day who recognized no deficiency in themselves, Jesus said, "They that be whole need not a physician, but they that are sick."[6] What He had to say would have little meaning to those who had no awareness of their need. This is still true today.

This sense of need may stem from many sources. It may come from a feeling of helplessness in the face of a crisis. It may come from a moral or psychological collapse. It may come from a dull throb of frustration or emptiness. But the point of man's extremity becomes the point of God's opportunity.

When a man, who is inwardly aware of his own insufficiency, acknowledges his need and willingly commits himself to God in Christ, as best he understands—that man experiences God for himself. It is not a commitment to propositions, but a commitment to a Person. That Person is Jesus Christ! The Biblical word for this commitment is "faith." Faith is the response of the total person to God. In this leap of faith there is no way to escape risk. Just as there was no way to escape risk when my wife and I married. We believed that we loved each other and that we meant what we said, ". . . for better or for worse . . . until death do us part." But, the only way we could be certain was to risk marriage. The only way we can be sure God is really there and really cares and will give us a new kind of life is to risk commitment. If He is not there, we have lost nothing. But if He is there, we have gained everything.

QUESTIONS

1. What do you consider to be the most important events which have shaped your life?
2. What mental snapshot or actual photograph do you have of yourself that you like best?
3. Do you believe that life can be different for you?
4. Do you know anyone who has changed significantly?
5. Have you ever recognized a restlessness in yourself?
6. Can you identify with any of the stages of rebellion discussed in this chapter? Have you ever come to grips with your own self-centeredness?
7. Have you ever felt utterly alone? What did you do?
8. If you could be certain of God's existence and of His love, would you want to know Him?
9. Have you ever read the four gospels in the New Testament (Matthew, Mark, Luke and John) to see what God is like in Jesus Christ or have you depended more on hearsay for your concept of Christ?
10. Can you see that God is the only center big enough for life?
11. Have you ever consciously committed as much of yourself as you could to as much of Christ as you understood? Would you like to *now*? Then do so!

CHAPTER 2

KEEPING UP THE APPEARANCES

Speaking the truth in love . . .

Things went well for a time after I made my start with Christ. Then some problems arose which I could not understand. I thought that becoming a Christian meant no more struggles—one became God's person and had it made. All of the witnesses that I heard spoke of successes in the Christian life. Consequently, if I said anything, it was only of a success, never of a failure. To admit that I had prayed for something earnestly and received no answer was, in my thinking, to deny faith in God.

There were, however, times when God seemed to act dramatically in my life and in the lives of those around me. One such time was during the serious illness of my uncle. The doctor had said that he would not live through the night. His two sons and I went across the street from our house into the cemetery nearby to be alone. There, under an oak tree, we wept, and through our tears we prayed for his life to be spared. After about three hours we walked back to the house to find that he had passed the crisis. The three of us were so amazed at what happened that we were unable to say anything about our experience for a long time.

The conversion of the man I worked for was another "success." I tried to live on that experience for a long time. He had made it plain to me that nothing religious would be brought up at work. My boss was a great guy and we became real friends. Three years later he told me he was coming to hear me share my witness at a small country church. I went to the church early. I walked down into a large pecan grove and prayed that God would bring this man to the church and that I would be able to communicate my faith to him. He had said several times before that he would come and hear me, yet he never had. I had tried to share my faith, but it never seemed to come out right. When I returned to the church there was only one other car there—it was his. That night his whole family accepted Christ, and for the next ten years he was a spiritual brother to me. He has since died, but the experiences we struggled through together were very meaningful times for me.

In the first church I pastored there was a couple who had tried for fourteen years to have a child. After a series of tests the doctor said that they would never be able to have children. Deeply disappointed over this, they talked with me about it. I didn't suggest to them that they pray for a child, because I feared that, if God did not answer, they would be disappointed again. However, I began to pray for them, and I am sure they prayed without my suggestion. Less than two months later they came to church one morning all excited. They were going to have a child, and the doctor had no explanation. I couldn't believe it. I told no one except my wife about my prayer.

One summer in that first pastorate we had a drought; there was no rain and the crops were dying. There were three deacons in that church who were like fathers to me. They were real and they cared about people. The four of us spent a great deal of time sharing and praying together about the needs of that little congregation. That particular summer, during the revival meeting, we asked God for rain to end the drought. It was a very meaningful week in the life of the church. On the last Sunday morning it started raining.

It rained so hard that when one of the deacons started home after church he had to park his car and wade the river for a half mile to get to the bridge to cross, so he could make it home. The next Sunday in our prayer time he said he felt that we had said one or two prayers too many for rain! But the drought was over, and the spirit of that rural congregation was high.

My faith was simple and, I'm sure, naive. I tried to live from one dramatic experience to the next. And the dramatic experiences, as I understood the dramatic, seemed to be too few and far between. I felt that, if something spectacular was not happening, my faith was weakening. As a result, I missed most of what was going on in the valleys, waiting to get back to the mountain. This is one reason, I am convinced, that our concepts of the Christian life are vitally important. We can never capture God in words and ideas, or fully comprehend the life He is giving us, but the Scriptures aid us in our understanding of God and the kind of life He has offered to us. To get away from the concrete, biblical revelation of what life should be is to cut ourselves adrift from the essentials.

I misunderstood conversion. I thought of conversion as a cure-all, which it seemed to be for awhile. Most of us live maybe six months or a year on the enthusiasm generated by our initial encounter with God. The initial stage of our blast-off with God seems to carry us along with almost no effort on our part. This is a part of God's care in protecting us, like a tender plant. The day comes for most of us, however, when we wake up with many of the same old problems—and a whole batch of new ones. A feeling of defeat comes, because we have misunderstood. But, we feel we had better fake it anyway. So, fake it we do! The moment we start falsifying our faith is the moment we lose our sense of excitement about being God's person. The biblical word for this fraudulence is "hypocrisy." The tragic aspect of hypocrisy is that it short-circuits our relationship with God and with each other and keeps us from being real.

To feel that, because we are Christians, we cannot get

angry or upset is to deny our humanity. Instead of accepting and dealing with these feelings, we take a deep breath and swallow them. The result is that we "stew in our own juice"—not a very good practice.

The apostle Paul kept his relationship to Simon Peter on the level. When Simon went to Antioch where Paul had been ministering, he found some sharp, newly-converted Greeks who greatly impressed him. Peter was having the time of his life in company with these Gentiles. Then some Judaizers from Jerusalem came and confronted Peter with their belief that a Gentile had to first become a Jew before he could really be in God's kingdom. Simon Peter bought their ideas and quickly segregated himself from the Gentile Christians. When Paul arrived and saw what had happened, he was angry. Paul thought it had been settled that salvation was by grace through faith and not by becoming, ceremonially, a Jew. Paul said, "I confronted Peter to his face and called him a role player (hypocrite)."[1] This turned out to be very redemptive for Simon. These men were not plaster saints. They were real flesh and blood people who made mistakes. Yet, in spite of their mistakes, these men turned the world upside down!

Conversion does not make us immune to personal conflicts or to the temptations that all men face. It does not immunize us against ups and downs in our spiritual pilgrimage, or cure us of our love of money or of our drive to look good to the other guy. In fact, conversion may actually intensify some of our problems.

What, then, does conversion mean? It means that we have started, but not finished. Now God has been allowed to get into our experience. The tap root of our rebellion has been cut. We now have resources within that we never had before, but we must live out this new relationship in our own skin. Conversion means that we are no longer alone. If someone grows up experiencing little love, there are problems created that no conversion will completely cure. God comes in to help that person work through the problems which this lack of love has produced. The miracle of

God is that He enables us to work through our problems in such a way that we gain character in the struggle. God changes our problems into opportunities for growth!

God does not call us to abandon our humanity. He comes to enable us to live with our humanity and to bring wholeness to it. At the point of accepting my own humanity, a new kind of growth is demanded. This is the "raw faith" stage. Our feelings may fluctuate, but if our commitment to Christ is real, He will see us through. However, the fact that He is in it with us does not eliminate struggle or seeming failure.

I have always been an idealist, wanting to eliminate all the problems so I could concentrate on enjoying life. I have been angry with myself and with my own immaturity. As far back as I can remember, I have wanted to hurry and grow up. I wanted to find the answers to all of my questions, work out all of my inner contradictions, and settle all of my conflicts, so at last I would be ready to live. I even tried to do this in the churches I pastored. It was my feeling that if we could just solve the personal problems of each member of the congregation and eliminate the problems in the congregation as a whole, then we could really be God's people in His world. Trying to accomplish this, I worked in one pastorate for five years without even taking a vacation. Every time one problem was solved, two others arose.

It seems that before conversion we try to play God for ourselves, and after conversion we try to play God for everyone else. I tried it and was a miserable flop. I had to face again the reality that something in me resists being totally dependent upon God. My pride wants me to achieve. But to see again that this is His deal and that I am His, and to relax and let Him take over was a tremendous relief. I took a vacation and enjoyed it. I rediscovered my family, which has turned out to be about the most significant thing that has ever happened to me. And what the Lord began to do in loving that church, when I gave it to Him, amazed me beyond words.

I had needed to hear a witness such as Paul gave in

II Corinthians 12. He said he had a problem that just kept bugging him. He prayed three times for it to be removed. God answered him by saying that His grace would enable him to live with his infirmity. Paul concluded that this problem was being used to make him aware of his total dependence upon God. It was in his weakness that God's strength was being revealed. Paul's response was, "I am most happy, then, to be proud of my weaknesses, in order to feel the protection of Christ's power over me. I am content with weaknesses, insults, hardships, persecutions, and difficulties for Christ's sake. For when I am weak, then I am strong."[2] Paul accepted his weaknesses as God's opportunity to make Himself known.

It is in the midst of our predicament that God is revealing Himself, and it is here that we must live out our faith. I am beginning to see the love and the wisdom of God in doing it His way. He is doing something infinitely greater than I would have ever asked Him to do. He is sharing His Life with me and giving me character that can never be taken away! Knowing this, I can afford to admit to myself and to others where I am in my pilgrimage. I can feel free to be discouraged when I am discouraged, and encouraged when I am encouraged. God is enabling me to accept myself and to live with myself, and in the process of this He is continually changing me.

Some have been concerned about the risk of being so honest. It is risky to remove our mask, especially our religious mask. One man said on a retreat, "You know, the thing that scares me most in trying to remove my mask is not what I will find, but what I won't find. I am afraid that I'll pull my mask down and there won't be anything there." This fear of losing our identity is very real. Jesus Christ, in becoming a man, has assured us that there is a real self within man worth redeeming.

Removing the mask also involves honesty in our relationships. There needs to be an open, authentic dialogue between people, especially between God's people, in which there is the kind of acceptance that we can express honesty and openness in our relationship. This is honesty with love, or "speaking the truth in love."[3] To speak the truth in love is to consider the other person. It was some time after I discovered this that something else spoke to me out of that Scripture. I am also to speak the truth about myself in love. I am not to pour out all of me on everyone who comes along, or maybe not on anyone. There are times when I need to talk about myself, and there are times when I should say little about myself. "In love" is the key to honesty, because love allows me to be aware of God's promptings.

Dr. Paul Tournier, a psychiatrist from Geneva, Switzerland, was asked during a conference at Earlham College how much openness one should practice with others. Dr. Tournier replied, "Be prepared to say it all but say only what you feel God leading you to say." Being prepared to say it all relieves us of our fear of being found out or exposed, so that we can respond to another in loving honesty without the fear of saying too much. In being prepared to say it all, we are also free to be silent when we should be. Love will keep us from simply parading our problems and will enable us to bear a hopeful witness. "We must speak the truth about ourselves in a spirit of love that we may grow up in every way in Christ."[4]

Removing our mask is risky, but it is equally risky not to remove our mask. To keep on trying to be what others expect us to be or want us to be, without ever coming to any real personhood, will lead to insanity. The truth is, the harder we try to please everyone, the more certain it is that we will please no one. The cry of our day is, "I've got to be me." Be yourself in Christ!

One man, after hearing some of these things, asked, "What will this do to my witness? How will this look to other people? My reply was, "You will seem more human." Something in us still wants to identify with God and be an exception.

There is a legitimate concern over how something I say or do will affect someone else. I do have a responsibility to my brother and his sensitivity. As Paul said, "If I eat meat and it offend my brother, then I will not eat meat."[5] This is legitimate to the degree that it involves my brother's sensitivity, but it is illegitimate if it produces phoniness and unreality in me. There will be unavoidable tension at this point. Maybe we can resolve some of this tension by asking ourselves, "What is our witness anyway?" We are not bearing witness to the fact that we have arrived. We are not, as a church, saying to the world, "We have achieved perfection; come over here and be like we are." We are saying, "Look, we are here because we have acknowledged that we cannot go it on our own. We need God's grace and forgiveness and help. We have not arrived, but we have started." Our witness to Christ is that we have found Someone who accepts us where we are and enables us to live with ourselves while He changes us. We have found in Christ Someone who has given us real hope of being different. The world is hungry for this kind of authentic witness!

In sharing only our seeming strengths, we may crush someone who is struggling for his very life. To share the weaknesses that Christ is enabling us to live with may give hope to a struggling person. Paul Tournier points out in *The Strong and the Weak:*

> The truth is that human beings are much more alike than they think. What is different is the external mask, sparkling or disagreeable, their outward reaction, strong or weak. These appearances, however, hide an identical inner personality . . . All men, in fact, are weak. All are weak because all are afraid. They are all afraid of being trampled underfoot. They are all afraid of their inner weakness being discovered. They all have secret faults; they all have a bad conscience on account of certain acts which they would like to keep covered up. They are all afraid of other men and of God, of themselves, of life and of death. What distinguishes men from each other is not their inner nature, but the way in which they react to this common distress.[6]

The real value for us is not our strong or weak reactions, but the use to which we put them in God's service.

There was a woman who had been in religious work for over twenty years who came to me for counseling. She was obviously upset. During our conversation she said that life had become so unbearable that she was contemplating suicide. As I tried to help her find some answers, she became hostile toward me. At one point she said, "I know the answers. I have been telling other people for over twenty years what the answers are. But my problem is that the answers don't work for me."

I decided to take a risk with her. I began to share a disillusioning experience that had come to me in my pastorate. I felt that the congregation and I, after some initial struggles, had grown into a real family. Old wounds of resentment had been healed, and the fellowship that our church family experienced was dynamic. Then I found myself facing indignation and resentment directed toward me because of my emphasis on the ministry of the laity. I could not understand the lack of tolerance on the part of some for something that was so meaningful to a large portion of the church.

I came to the place where I felt that if this was the best that any of us could expect from ourselves or others, I wanted out. I even doubted the validity of the Gospel. My first reaction was to quit—to give up the ministry—even though I had felt, and still felt, a call to the ministry. I told this woman how, in agony, I had wrestled with my dilemma. My discouragement was such that, for a long period of time, I was in real turmoil. Then I felt guilty about my own indecisiveness. I could not accept it. Finally, I began to realize what I had been doing—I was rejecting my own humanity and the humanity of others. With this realization came some acceptance of my struggle. That acceptance relieved the sharp anxiety and allowed a new perspective to come into focus.

As I shared my struggle, she began to relax. At one point she burst in and said, "I didn't know a Christian could have that kind of struggle." To which I replied, "I didn't know it either. And that was part of my problem."

It has been more than two years since our first conversation. That woman is giving herself to other people in ministry as she never had in her twenty years before this crisis. Christ ministered to this woman out of my weakness, not out of my strength!

With God's help we can be free from having to keep up appearances.

QUESTIONS

1. How do you feel about being honest and open with others? Is there a right way and a wrong way?
2. Do you have any feelings which are unacceptable to you? What do you do with them?
3. Do you seek to live from one great experience to another, or do you seek to keep everything routine?
4. Do you ever find yourself struggling? What do your struggles mean to you? Do you fight, flee or face them?
5. Have you recognized, accepted and affirmed your own humanity with both its potential and brokenness?
6. How do you react to the unwholeness in others around you?
7. Have you ever experienced God using your weakness to help another?
8. What does the writer mean about one's witness becoming more human? How human is your witness?
9. What are some of the masks you wear?
10. What effect would there be on you if you really believed God accepted you as you are and wanted to bring you to complete wholeness?

CHAPTER 3

WHAT ABOUT MY PAST?

If we confess our sins, he is faithful and just to forgive us our sins, and to cleanse us from all unrighteousness . . .

It has been said that our past follows us, but it does much more than simply follow us. It lives with us. Each person is the sum total of all he has experienced, thought and dreamed, plus all that God has made him. This growth is essential for continuity in personality. This essential continuity in our experience keeps us from waking up each morning like a newborn infant, having to learn everything all over again. For this reason we can be grateful that our past lives with us.

Many strengths (which most of us probably take for granted) come from our past. For example, my parents built into me a strong value system. We just did not, "tell stories" around our house. My dad let us know that, if his arm held out, he was not going to raise a liar. His arm held out long enough to get across his point.

Right beside the positive elements of our past are the negative aspects. None of us has escaped being crippled some way in our past. We were born into a world marred by sin. Our parents were sinners, and so were their parents before them. The earlier we can recognize this and can forgive our parents for their sins against us, the sooner we can be free of that handicap. In forgiving them we can have hope that our children, when they recognize our sins against them, will be able to forgive us. Forgiveness is an aspect of love which is necessary to keep us from destroying each other, and which makes possible healthy relationships.

The good news of the Christian message is that Jesus Christ comes to save the whole person, including our past. Our past cannot be re-lived; it is forever our "past." But, the way we relate to it can be changed, and for most of us, it must be changed! This has been demonstrated to me both in my own experience and in the experience of those whom I have counseled.

One middle-aged man came to me for counseling. He had been so dominated by his father (who had been dead for years) that he was immobilized in his own business. He was a very wealthy man, but because of this domination he was extremely fearful of his own decisions. His father had taken the risks in the business; he had been successful, and had made sure his son knew it. When the father died, the business became the son's. For years the son had limped along, unable to operate the business as his own. It was still his "father's" business. When he made a deal, he was afraid to check it out to see how much profit he had made. He was always sure he had made the wrong decision and had lost money. This attitude was creating tremendous problems in his marriage and with his children, to say nothing of the inner "hell" that he was experiencing. The night he finally came to some real self-understanding and opened this bondage from the past to Jesus Christ was the night that real deliverance began. He was excited as he began to talk about the changes he was going to make in that business and how he was going to expand it. He made me think of a little boy whose dream had just come true. Needless to say, things have been different in his family life as well. He was not freed from all adversity, but he was free to begin to be his own person in the midst of the struggle.

There comes a time in our growing up that, if our relationship to our parents is to be healthy, it must no longer be a parent-child relationship, but a peer relationship—a face-to-face relationship. In one church where I was speaking about Christ enabling us to mature in our relationships, a grandmother shared in privacy the domination that her mother still had over her. Just getting married and growing older does not guarantee that the umbilical cord is cut. But, for the sake of all concerned, including the mother, the cord must be cut or life will be stifled. This woman had been stifled, but that night she found freedom similar to that of the businessman I told you about.

We are fortunate if we have known love and security in growing up. Life will not be the terrifying prospect that it is for those who have known little love or security. In the '60s a young man on a retreat helped me realize the tremendous significance that the emotional climate of our past has in our experience. He was a twenty-four-year-old hippie. All weekend the resource people on this retreat had been trying to communicate to him that God loved him. In fact, during the free time on that Saturday afternoon, six or eight of us spent the entire time in dialogue with him—which was what he wanted.

He would demand, "What is love? Love is impersonal and abstract. It's nothing more than an idea or ideal."

We would reply, "No, love is very personal and concrete. It was embodied in perfection in Jesus of Nazareth."

Little progress was made in this dialogue session, but later, in another small group discussion, this young man said, "The earliest memory I have is of my dad holding my mom in the doorway, slamming her head on one side of the doorway and then on the other . . . I have never known love from any human being. I guess the closest I ever came to knowing love was from a girl in high school, but this relationship did not last long." Then it hit me like a bolt of lightning. We had been trying to communicate "love" in words, and he had no previous experience to which he could relate. We must experience love before we can truly understand love.

At this point I feel it is necessary to make clear the fact

that we are not simply victims of our circumstances. Our circumstances affect us deeply, but we still have some freedom in choosing our response to those circumstances. In a very real sense each person chooses his own destiny. This eliminates blind fate and offers us hope of change, if we so desire it. History is full of people who overcame great odds in carving out a significant place for themselves in life. This means there is no constructive place for self-pity. Regardless of how unfavorable my circumstances may have been, I am as I am partly because I have chosen to be so. And my only reason for staying as I am is that I refuse to be different. I may cleave to my problem to gain pity, or to get from others what I want, or to avoid being accountable or acting responsibly. In this way, I deny my own selfhood, and negate the power of God to cure me.

Jesus asked a man who had been sick for thirty-eight years, "Do you want to get well?"[1] It was a long time before I understood the import of this question. Surely anyone who had been sick so long would want to get well. Not necessarily! Some of us seek by sickness to retreat from life and responsibility. Psychology is helping us to see that much of our physical disease is first a mental or emotional disease. When life becomes too much to cope with, we can withdraw from it all by becoming ill. This may be the best thing for us at that particular time. However, continued refusal to face our real problems so that they can be resolved is the destructive element. Dealing with reality eliminates the necessity for escape. All of us, without exception, have developed escapes which enable us to live with the unpleasantness of our past. Until we are able to face the particulars of our past with integrity, we must elude the pain that recalling them produces. It would not be wise for any of us suddenly to abandon all our releases. What is wise is to recognize our escape mechanisms—such as continual illnesses, excessive talking, craving for long periods of sleep, criticism, preachments to others—as just that. To recognize our escapes for what they are, to try to find out what we are trying to avoid and why, and to commit it to Jesus Christ for help in resolving the deeper problem—this is to face our past with integrity.

The real question here for us is, "Do we really want to be made whole?" In John 5, the man whom Jesus confronted with this question did not answer in the affirmative. He began to make excuses for why he had not been healed, which is quite human. Yet Jesus did for him what he needed—He healed him. The religious leaders saw this man as he was on his way home, carrying his bed. When they questioned him about laboring on the Sabbath, he was completely unwilling to take any responsibility for his actions. He laid the blame on the One who healed him and who had told him to take up his bed and walk. What ingratitude! Yet, there is love in Christ's action. He is forcing that man back into a responsible role rather than leaving him to his self-pity, which was more destructive than his physical illness.

That same Christ is our Disturber as well. He constantly seeks to push us and bring us back into the mainstream of life. Sometimes I wish He didn't love me with that great a love. His love refuses to leave me where I am. Yet, I see that my only hope is that His great love will never fail. We want and need love, but we fear great love. Little love may give me some feeling of worth, but love as great as the love of God-in-Christ woos from me the sovereignty of my own life. And, the last thing I will surrender into the hand of God is *me*. Yet, that is the first and the only thing He asks.

Another way we relate to our past is to seal off segments and try to forget that they ever happened. This is as futile as discovering we have cancer and trying to get rid of it by pretending that it is non-existent. The cancer continues its ugly work, and so does the unresolved guilt from our past. The energy spent in concealing our past is energy taken from creative life in the present. And this unresolved guilt from our past is a major source of anxiety. We try to forget, but our deep mind never forgets. We try to keep the lid on our past, fearing someone or something might suddenly expose us. This creates an uneasinesss which never leaves us. But if we would just open the corridors of our past and let the

Living God move through them—forgiving the guilt, healing the hurt and making us free from the fear of being found out—then we could face the present with its opportunities and problems in an up-to-date relationship with Jesus Christ. What hope this would offer. Yet there is still fear and pain in opening our past to God.

As Cecil Osborne has pointed out in his book *The Art of Understanding Yourself,* there is a tension between the need to reveal and the need to conceal.[2] This was brought home to me in a humorous way during a week-long conference at Laity Lodge at which I was speaking. Arnold Holley, a friend of mine, was working at Laity that summer. We had been mistaken for each other several times before. (In college we had a class together. Once when I was to give a report, I was introduced as Creath, but with Arnold's background information). At this particular conference, a psychologist there for the week was involved in a ministry in which Arnold was interested. Arnold asked him for a conference sometime during the week. A day or two later this counselor and I were eating lunch together, and he suggested that I come over to his room after lunch to talk. I took it for granted he wanted to discuss something about the week's activities, so after lunch I went to his room. In a very casual manner he sat down facing me and asked, "Creath, what do you think we ought to talk about?" I suddenly felt panic. There was a definite tension between the need to reveal and the need to conceal. I thought this fellow had been observing me all week and had evidently seen some quirk in my personality which he felt needed to be changed. I didn't want to give him any more information than he already had, so I replied, "I don't know, what do you think we ought to talk about?" I can't tell you what a relief it was for me when he realized he was talking to the wrong fellow! Later I asked myself, "Why shouldn't I be free enough in my relationship to Jesus Christ to be open without such panic? He comes to bring us the kind of love that casts out fear and dissolves anxiety." I began to realize that there were parts of my past that I had been unable to offer to God wholly, so that I could accept His forgiveness and, in turn, forgive myself.

There is a biblical word for offering something unacceptable to God for Him to deal with. It is "confession." The Scriptures declare, "If we confess our sins, he is faithful and just to forgive us our sins, and to cleanse us from all unrighteousness."[3] This matter of confession is more than simply acknowledging that we are guilty of something. It means to agree with God concerning a particular sin; to agree in the sense that we feel some of the agony and distress that He feels over this rebellious action on our part. This kind of confession comes with genuine repentance. We are dependent upon the Spirit of God who enables us to confess and repent of our sins. Apart from God's help, the best we can do is wallow in remorse.

There is a tremendous difference in repentance and remorse. This is illustrated in Simon Peter and Judas Iscariot. Simon Peter and Judas Iscariot both blew it. Simon cursed and denied that he knew the Lord. Judas sold Him out for thirty pieces of silver. One went out and wept bitterly; the other went out and hanged himself. Simon turned back in repentance; Judas turned away in remorse. Remorse is concerned with the consequences; repentance is concerned with the relationship. It is remorse to say, "Oh, Lord, forgive me and eliminate the consequences." It is repentance to say, "Oh, Lord, forgive me and cure me, regardless of the consequences. And, if need be, double the consequences to cure me." One man said, "I'm not about to pray like that." I responded, "Neither am I. Only God can enable us to pray like that. But when we want to be made whole and not simply to escape the consequences, then God will enable us to utter such a prayer."

At one of our retreats there was a woman who seemed very religious, but somehow it was hard to relate to her. She was tough on everyone, showing little sympathy or love. Later she came for counseling. In our conversation she said, "I was having an affair with another man. I think that the reason I was acting so religious on the retreat was that I was trying to compensate for my guilt."

There are two ways we can try to deal with our guilt:

either we attempt to pay for it, or we find forgiveness. There is no constructive way we can pay for guilt or compensate for it. We may try to conceal it, but it will poison our whole life unless it is resolved.

In II Samuel the story is told of David's great sin. He took another man's wife and arranged for her husband to be killed. He was the King. Who could reprimand him? No one had to. David's own witness of this experience is found in Psalm 32. "When I kept silence, my bones waxed old through my roaring all the day long. For day and night thy hand was heavy upon me: my moisture is turned into the drought of summer."[4] David tried to conceal his guilt, but inwardly it was tearing him apart. The Lord sent Nathan to help him acknowledge his guilt and get it out where something redemptive could be done.

Nathan told David a story about a rich man who had everything, and a poor man who had only one ewe lamb. When a traveler came, the rich man spared his own flock, but took the poor man's one lamb for the traveler. David's anger was kindled. His reaction was very human. We hate most vigorously the evil in others that we secretly recognize in ourselves. David told Nathan that this man would pay, and asked who he was. Nathan answered, "Thou art the man."[5] What David feared most had happened. He was exposed! His response to that exposure was one of agonizing repentance. Though his sin was not without consequences, from his repentance came deliverance. Psalm 51 is David's prayer of repentance, and Psalm 32 is his witness to the sweetness of forgiveness; "Blessed is he whose transgression is forgiven, whose sin is covered. Blessed is the man unto whom the Lord imputeth not iniquity, and in whose spirit there is no guile."[6] Healing comes only with forgiveness!

We must not only accept God's forgiveness, but we must also forgive ourselves. If we feel we have to ask God twice to pardon us for the same thing, then we have not forgiven ourselves. God forgave us the first time we asked, but we do not feel relief because of our reluctance to exonerate ourselves. Sometimes we have to have another person help us make forgiveness real. Some may be able to go out in solitude and confess their sin to God alone and come back with a deep sense of forgiveness. But since we were not made to live in solitude, most of us need another person to hear our confession to God to make our confession more sobering—and to make God's acceptance and forgiveness seem more real.

In my last pastorate there was a couple who were having marital difficulties. Part of the problem was an inner barrier which the wife could not break through. There was something in her past for which she felt extreme guilt, and she had never been able to experience forgiveness, pray as she would. This woman and my wife became close friends. One night this woman, unable to discuss openly the source of her guilt, wrote on a piece of paper what she had done and what she was now offering to God for forgiveness. She then handed the paper to my wife to read while she sat and wept. It was out! Now she had offered it to God in the company of another. A deep sense of forgiveness came. At last that woman was free to be herself! The change in her was so remarkable that her husband shared with me that he felt he had a new wife, and that this new wife was more lovely than the girl he had married seven years earlier. That's the miracle of God!

Not only does Christ bring us the kind of forgiveness that enables us to accept our past and to be free of its bondage. He also uses that past-given-to-Him in His redemptive purpose. I saw this in the experience I related earlier of my own struggle over whether I would stay in the ministry or not. Up until that time I had not been aware of any tremendous inner struggle. The only real struggle I had recognized had been an external one, which turned out to be more like an adventure. There had been some family opposition to my becoming a Christian, and, later, to my becoming a minister. Yet never had I known any deep inner agony. Out of a disillusive experience with my pastorate came a period of deep doubt about the validity of the Gospel and what was transpiring in my own life. Some of the things which I had taken as second-hand information were being hammered out in my own experience.

I also interpret this experience as preparation for the counseling ministry into which I have been thrust. It was not the way I would have chosen. I would have said, "Lord, send me to school for a course in counseling, but don't take me through the agony of an inner struggle." Before this experience, which lasted in varying degrees for the better part of two years, I would listen to people as they poured out their inner feelings and struggles, but without any understanding. They just needed more faith, I thought, never dreaming that they needed someone to walk through these shadows with them. Since that period in my own life, I understand as never before, some of the lonely, agonizing battles that many people fight.

God comes to redeem the whole man. Why not give Him our past?

QUESTIONS

1. Can you relate to both the assets and liabilities inherent in the reality of our "past living with us"?
2. Have you ever consciously examined your past—relationships and experiences—which have shaped your life? Did you find the need to forgive and be forgiven?
3. Are you carrying any unhealed wounds from your past? Do you want to get well?
4. Is your relationship with your parents a peer-relationship yet?
5. Why is there so much tension between your need to reveal and your need to conceal?
6. Is confession a regular part of your experience?
7. Is there a difference in true guilt and false guilt? Do your guilt feelings stem primarily from what you have done or from a general feeling of "worthlessness"? How can we deal with guilt?
8. How can God use your brokenness in a redemptive way?

CHAPTER 4

WHAT ABOUT MY FUTURE?

But seek ye first the kingdom of God, and his righteousness; and all these things shall be added unto you . . .

We must come to terms with our future as well as our past if we are to be free and open to life in the present. We must come to terms with our future to satisfy our desire for security and purpose. One of the strongest drives of the human psyche is to find something to undergird life— something that will never fail, that will sustain us even in eternity. For this reason, nothing material will suffice ultimately, for the things we can count, touch and see are only temporal.

Even though we need a sense of economic security, economic security without a sense of personal security ceases to be even economic security. In one of our Prayer Therapy groups we experienced something humorous in this area. It turned out to be very redemptive. This group of people had a wide range of social and economic status. There was one wealthy man who shared with the group his deep sense of insecurity, which was making his life unbearable. He feared financial upset and was exceedingly afraid of others' opinions of him. He said that sometimes he would go to a party, look in the window to see who was there, and then feel so insecure that he would get back in his car and go back home rather than face the people.

Some of those very people were in this group. One by one they began to share their fear of him. Because he was a man of wealth and power they felt inferior in his presence. There began to be laughter in the group as the sharing proceeded. It was laughter of relief. We found that we were alike, with similar insecurities. We were relieved, because we no longer had to fear each other or hide from each other. We had both our own humanity and God's acceptance in common—and we knew it.

This man experienced such freedom in the group that night that he was able to take the lead in helping the rest of us open up in the remainder of our sessions together.

Some have felt that the reason for the tremendous sense of insecurity in our day is the instability of our modern world. But that instability only magnifies for us our own basic insecurity. History bears witness to the fact that this world has bever been very stable. Wars and rumors of war, change and revolution have been a steady diet for the human race. Neither things nor circumstances can give us a deep sense of personal security. Things can be taken from us and circumstances can change. This is not to minimize the significance of the material in our experience, or the importance of our circumstances. They compose the arena in which we live out our faith. But we must recognize clearly that security has always been the dominion of the inner self.

The primary reason for our insecurity is our own finiteness. All of experience bears witness to our limitations, with the final witness being death. Being finite would not be so disturbing if we were not trying to play the role of the Infinite. Our alienation from God becomes the aggravating element in our sense of personal safety. As long as God is not the integrating center of our life, there is no way to escape a deep sense of personal jeopardy. We are out of harmony with our own psyche, and this disharmony creates terrific insecurity. Some assurance may come from one's home, job or reputation. But these cannot suffice for ultimate security.

A few years ago I shared my faith with a man who, because of our relationship, was very open to me, but who had no sense of his need for God. He was young and brilliant, with tremendous drive to achieve. And he was achieving in everything he attempted. Life held great promise for him. Two years later I received word that he wanted to see me. He had found out that he had an incurable disease. All the things which had given him a sense of meaning and security were shattered. He reminded me of our past conversation and asked me to tell him more. After a time of sharing together, he committed himself to Jesus Christ. In the face of his own limitation, he reached out for the One who would give him meaning and security even in death.

There are about as many secondary sources of insecurity as there are disabling experiences. To grow up in an insecure home with little love, or to be the object of a critical attitude, or simply to be taken for granted adds to one's sense of insecurity. Failing to be an achiever in a society that demands achievers also produces anxiety. I am convinced that healing, at this level, begins with finding ultimate security. To become confident as a person is to be free to begin working through our disabling experiences. Otherwise, we may hide or fight those disablers with little success.

Many ills arise from our insecurity. Greed is one. The more a person gets, the more he wants or dreams of getting. This insatiable drive for more and more results in his deriving less and less pleasure from what he already has. A fearful person cannot afford to be generous with himself or with his possessions. He must hoard everything and dominate others whenever possible. A man who had spent forty-five years in religious work said to me, "Son, if you are going to stay in the ministry, you'll have to develop a hide like an alligator." This man had a tremendous sense of insecurity and found it most difficult to be generous with people. He had insulated himself against everything and everyone. The tragic thing was that he had also insulated himself against love, while trying to govern others from a safe distance. Perhaps the little girl's prayer would be a fitting reminder to those of us in the community of faith, "Oh, Lord, make the bad people good and the good people nice."

A paralyzing fear of the unknown can squelch life in us. It blocks the full expression of our potential. As one layman put it on a retreat, "It's like living with your brakes on. You're not going very far and you are burning yourself out in the process."

In one of my pastorates, there was a young farmer whose farm was so unproductive that he had to borrow money every year to make his crop. This man participated in a small group fellowship in the church, and in that group he came to some startling discoveries about himself and about God. He began to realize that perhaps he had committed himself to a religious tradition and not to Jesus Christ. As this began to clear up for him, he said, "One day as I was driving home, I looked at my farm and said to myself, 'Well, I've been blind spiritually for a long time without recognizing it, maybe I have also been blind to my vocational potential.'" From the security in his own Christian pilgrimage and from the fellowship of that group he became an adventurer in his vocation. Now free to think in new categories, he began to venture into some new areas, and in nine years he built a quarter of a million dollar business. His fear of the unknown had limited his vision and kept him from achieving to his fullest capacity.

I've felt the pangs of insecurity—looking at the future and wondering what is ahead, while feeling keenly the responsibility of a wife and three children. Could I be an adequate husband and father and minister? Could I make it as a man? Our roles demand a sense of well-being both for today and tomorrow if we are to fill them adequately. The question that comes to us at this point is, "How can we have a sense of security about today and tomorrow when we are not in charge of the show?" With the limitations of today and with the future out of our hands, how can we feel secure? The answer cannot be found in word meanings, but in the kind of relationship with the Living God that creates a radical trust in Him. This complete trust the Bible calls "faith." The problem most of us encounter here is that we prefer not to be such riskers. We would like to move slowly into faith without letting go of our old efforts at security. But the more complete the abandonment of ourselves, including our future, to Jesus Christ, the more profound our security.

Someone will inevitably think of this radical trust in Jesus Christ as fanaticism, but the opposite is true. A fanatic is one who is basically uncertain, and who has to bolster his own certainty by forcing others to accept his position. The man who responds in faith (an outright commitment of his whole being to Jesus Christ) can allow others the freedom to choose their own course. Out of concern, he bears a witness to them, but how they choose to respond to that witness is not his problem.

In one retreat with a group of young people, the resource personnel gave a clear and winsome witness to the transforming power of Jesus Christ. With absolutely no pressure from anyone these young men and women were left to risk their life with this Christ. In the final session we had a time to recapitulate what had happened, positively or negatively, during the weekend. As we moved around the room one young man said, "I don't know whether this is proper or not, but I would like for everyone here to bow their heads and be my witness while I invite Jesus Christ into my life." With that, he did ask Jesus Christ into his life. Another young man, when it was his turn to share his impressions, did the same. After we had been completely around the room, hearing each one in turn, we were ready to conclude the meeting. Suddenly, a boy blurted out, "I've already had my turn but I failed to do what I really wanted to do. I, too, would like for everyone here to be my witness, as I invite Christ into my life." During all of this time something was happening to every one of us. Late on the Monday night following the retreat, one of these young men called me, so excited that he could not talk fast enough to tell me what he wanted. He said, "A group of us got together tonight and six other guys committed their lives to Jesus

Christ." This experience helped me to see again that we can trust God with the results!

We must commit our future to Jesus Christ in concrete terms, not just in theoretical. Sixteen years ago a group of laymen from Dallas and East Texas came to me with a proposition. (At that time I was in the midst of the most meaningful ministry of my life. I had no desire to leave my pastorate.) These laymen had experienced an encounter with Jesus Christ, and they were anxious to be a part of His redemptive enterprise in the world. They had a dream of trying to help other laymen like themselves find an exciting relationship with Jesus Christ. These men were active in their local churches, but they wanted to do more than they had been doing. I knew they were serious. I had been involved in a Bible study in Dallas with them for almost a year. There had been as many as 127 adults in one home for this Bible Study, and some of those people would stay most of the night asking questions. I have never ceased to be amazed at the deep hunger, so obvious in our day, for something meaningful.

These laymen invited me to come as their "equipper" and to help them in their lay ministry. The possibilities were staggering to me, but at that point they were only possibilities. I was secure where I was, in an established and acceptable form of ministry. These men were inviting me into a new frontier. I wanted to try it, but could I afford to risk it? Could I minister to these men as an equipper?

I talked with a close friend about my fears and he, seeing deeper than I realized at the time, said, "Why not risk it with them? You really don't have anything to lose, but a superficial security." How true! Why allow the fear of making a mistake keep us from venturing? After all, the only mistake that is fatal, from which there is no recovery, is the failure to venture with Jesus Christ. Why live with such reserve, with our throttle only half open? I have been so cautious at times and moved with such reserve that, had I bumped into anything, it would never have been noticed. I could have just backed up and gone around. Why not engage in life with intensity and quit dabbling? Why not risk it all with God in abandon?

I decided to risk it. I prayed, "Lord, this is Your deal, I hope; if it's not, I'm giving it to You. Whatever comes of this venture and of me and my family in it, is up to You. As best I know, I am committing all of us into Your hands. If it lasts a week, or twenty years, I give You thanks for giving me a shot at it." From time to time I have felt uncertain, but basically this venture has been the most relaxed and freeing of my whole life. The way the Lord has used these men in ministering to me and to others has been a continual source of encouragement. I am experiencing at a deeper level, yet not without fears, the security that I had talked about for years.

Part of our ministry is retreats for personal renewal. For years we used borrowed facilities. At one point we thought we were ready to build our Lodge, but the plans fell through. One of the directors came to me and asked me why I wasn't upset. He said, "You've got more to lose than any of us in this, and I can't understand why it doesn't bother you more." I hadn't thought of it in that way, but being unable to carry through on our plans was no threat to me, and I hadn't even realized it. I said to this director, "No, I don't have anything to lose. I had nothing to start with, and whatever I have now is not of my doing." To taste freedom from anxiety and disappointment in this deal, which is contrary to my nature, was an indication to me that perhaps God had taken me up on my prayer.

One of our directors, after a week-end retreat, said he felt impelled to push ahead with the construction of our facilities, confident that the finances would become available. They did. These men are riskers, and the Lord is teaching me something in their company.

Kaleo Lodge has now been built and has met with unbelievable success in being a place where men and women can explore *God's Good News* without pressure of any kind.

If we build our lives on something we have to protect, we can never be free to take a chance. The same young farmer, mentioned earlier in this chapter, came to realize that, if he built his life on his farming operation, he could never risk being creative. After he began to come alive as God's person, he flew over his farm one day. He said that, as he looked down at that small operation which had been his whole world and the foundation on which he was building his life, he realized how foolish it was to build his life on something so small. He said, "From the air that farm was one little plot of land in the midst of a multitude of others. A man made in the image of God cannot afford to tie his whole life to something so insignificant." We all need to have a view from the air of the things we count so important. Apart from God, everything is too small.

We must build our lives upon Jesus Christ, who "is the visible expression of the invisible God. He existed before creation began, for it was through Him that everything was made, whether spiritual or material, seen or unseen. Through Him, and for Him, also, were created power and dominion, ownership and authority. In fact, every single thing was created through, and for, Him. He is both the first principle and the upholding principle of the whole scheme of creation."[1] Then we can be free to venture far beyond our limited courage in every area of life. By faith, this Christ becomes our contemporary. He is not only God breaking into history two thousand years ago, but He becomes God involved in our history today.

In what the church has called the Great Commission,[2] the resurrected Christ gives His disciples the tremendous task of making willing learners of all nations. What an assignment! But He declares that they are not to tackle this job alone. He promises to be with them always. Can you imagine Jesus Christ, through the Holy Spirit with us, having all the resources of heaven above and earth beneath to bring into our little lives, freeing us and empowering us for the adventure of life? It is little wonder that Paul wrote, "If God be for us, who can be against us?"[3] This was not preachment with him; it was reality. Paul spoke from experience. From his prison cell he wrote:

> Don't worry about anything, but in all your prayers ask God for what you need, always asking him with a thankful heart. And God's peace, which is far beyond human understanding, will keep your hearts and minds safe, in Christ Jesus . . . I know what it is to be in need, and what it is to have more than enough. I have learned this secret, so that anywhere, at any time, I am content, whether I am full or hungry, whether I have too much or too little. I have the strength to face all conditions by the power that Christ gives me.[4]

None of us can know what our immediate future may hold, but we can know the One who holds our future, and that is infinitely better.

QUESTIONS

1. How can we really be free to live creatively in the present?
2. What is security? Would you describe yourself as being basically secure or insecure?
3. Share an area in which you have some feelings of insecurity. In relating to people? To strangers? To new situations? In lack of knowledge or education? In achievement? In productivity? In acceptance? In economics or social status?
4. Are you afraid of people with great wealth or prestige?
5. How do you feel toward those who have less than you and who cannot enhance your position?
6. What are some of the secondary sources of insecurity in your life?
7. How do you feel about the future? Your future?
8. Is it easy for you to risk?
9. What has been your greatest risk?
10. Can you see how the lack of security will either increase your need for attention from others or will cause you to hide?

11. What are some ways you attempt to hide your insecurity? In timidity? Arrogance? Indifference?
12. What are your status symbols? What gives you a feeling of security and worth?
13. Does the Christian faith offer any real security? What? How?

CHAPTER 5

THE NEED FOR SELF-ACCEPTANCE

Thou shalt love thy neighbor as thyself.

For years I missed something highly significant in the two great commandments that Christ gave us. A lawyer had asked Christ to tell him which was the greatest commandment in the Law. Christ responded by simplifying the whole Law for him. The two commandments which contain the essence of all the prophets and the Law are, "Thou shalt love the Lord thy God with all thy heart, and with all thy soul, and with all thy mind. This is the first and great commandment. And the second is like unto it, Thou shalt love thy neighbor as thyself."[1] I had interpreted these two commandments as loving God with your whole being and loving your neighbor *instead* of yourself. That sounds very noble, perhaps, at first glance, but in it I was failing to be true either to God, my neighbors or myself. I had adopted the pietist attitude which tried to ignore self, hoping he would fall in line or go away completely. He never went away, for which I am profoundly grateful, because that *self* is *me*. Trying to relate to myself in such an unrealistic way was creating tremendous conflicts and problems. I was trying to negate my life, which is contrary to God's purpose and to my own well-being.

The deepest drive of human personality is survival. This drive for survival is far deeper than a simple biological reflex. It is the drive to survive as a person—as a human being, not an animal. We desperately struggle to keep from becoming insignificant, from just being a number or a name without a face. When a person does lose his sense of identity and significance, he either rebels or he crawls back to the animalistic level of existence to try to survive there.

While in India on a study tour I witnessed the results of a religion that seeks to negate the person. To the Hindu, the ultimate meaning of life is to be liberated, or released from the "wheel of life." He works to come to that place where he is no longer involved in individual existence, but is unified with and absorbed into deity. Hinduism denies personhood to the degree that if one refuses to accept his lot in life and seeks to better himself, he sins greatly.

Christianity affirms life and personal identity. Christ said that He came to give us "abundant life." He came not to free us *from* life, but to free us *for* life. He increases one's individuality. He gives us both the sense of our own worth and a sense of deep interrelatedness with others. We become part of a caring community!

The truth is that I cannot love God or my neighbor until I come to a proper love of myself. We cannot give to another what we do not have. This may sound incompatible with the Scripture that says, "If any man will come after me, let him deny himself, and take up his cross, and follow me. For whosoever will save his life shall lose it: and whosoever will lose his life for my sake shall find it;"[2] or the Scripture, "Knowing this that our old man is crucified with him;"[3] or again, "I am crucified with Christ."[4] Our problem is that we did not read far enough in these passages before we gave our interpretation. In the section from Matthew, Jesus went on to say, "Will a man gain anything if he wins the whole world but loses his life? Of course not! There is nothing a man can give to regain his life."[5] This does not sound as if Christ wants us to nullify ourselves.

We need to ask, "What self is it that we are to deny?"

We can translate Matthew 16:25 as, "If a man *selfishly* grasps his own life he will lose it." We come to personal realization and fulfillment only when we are no longer the center of our own life. In the Romans passage, the "old man is crucified . . . that . . .we should not serve sin." The "old man" mentioned is again the destructive, self-centered self. In the Galatians passage, Paul declares his identification with Christ and his life of faith in Christ, "who loved me and gave himself for me." There is no New Testament passage that teaches that Christ wants to obliterate us or reduce us to nonentities. He purposes to destroy the false self created by sin, and to liberate the true self made in the image of God for fulfillment and fellowship with God. To realize this was like a breath of fresh air.

People in the area of psychology have discovered this age-old truth, and have stressed the absolute necessity of coming to a "proper self-image," "self-acceptance" or "healthy egoism." These are interrelated. The way a person sees himself, or imagines himself to be, determines his conduct and the extent of his abilities.

I ran track in high school. There were three of us in our district who ran the hundred-yard dash with a ten-second timing. My sense of inferiority caused me to see myself as third man. For three years I ran third when we competed against each other, although in other meets or in practice my time was the same as theirs. Visualizing myself as third man kept me third man. Then in my senior year, at a college practice meet, our best 440-yard man was running against time in practice. I imagined I could beat him. He had already started running before the coach told me to catch him. I pulled off my warm-ups and beat him. The college track coach offered me a scholarship based on that one run. After that I saw myself differently and that enabled me to move from third man to first man in track my senior year.

The Scripture declares, "For as he thinketh in his heart, so is he."[6] What a person thinks or imagines, good or bad, becomes as much a part of him as the things that actually happen. Even the way a person reflects upon the experiences in his life determines the way these events will affect him. If a person interprets a certain incident as one of rejection, whether it was or not, he acts on his interpretation. It could not be more real to him if it had actually been rejection. A person's inner world dictates and determines the way in which he sees and relates to his outer world.

Dr. Maxwell Maltz, a famous plastic surgeon, after years of experience in changing the physical faces of men, wrote:

> It was as if personality itself had a "face." This non-physical "face of personality" seemed to be the real key to personality change. If it remained scarred, distorted, "ugly," or inferior, the person himself acted out this role in his behavior regardless of the changes in physical appearance. If this "face of personality" could be reconstructed, if old emotional scars could be removed, then the person himself changed, even without facial plastic surgery. Once I began to explore this area, I found more and more phenomena which confirmed the fact that the "self image," the individual's mental and spiritual concept or "picture" of himself, was the real key to personality and behavior.[7]

The concept a person has of himself deep within determines the kind of person he becomes. When my image changed of what a minister is to be, my own image changed. I changed and so did my ministry. It was a tremendously freeing experience.

In a youth retreat we asked the group to write down how they thought their peers saw them, how their parents saw them, and how they saw themselves. A girl wrote that her peers saw her as "a shy person who seems to be a snob—can be fun to be with, but is often unsure"; her parents saw her as "their darling daughter who must be protected at all costs from the bad wolves who inhabit the world—every day she receives a lecture on how she should act—they seem to feel she has no mind or judgment of her own"; she sees herself as "a scared person who truly doesn't know herself very well. She is shy and that is often why she seems a snob. She is unsure of herself in the world. It is often difficult for her to make friends—but she rarely loses the ones she has made. She is too frank and blunt many times, even though she doesn't mean to hurt the feelings of others." A boy wrote that his peers "probably think I'm a put on, a fake"; that his parents "think I never do anything bad. Well, hardly ever"; and of himself he said, "I think I am a slob and a fake." The things they shared as the weekend continued proved that they were being true to their own self image.

Since our own inner world dictates and determines how we see and relate to our outer world, if that inner world is out of contact with reality, then we will be out of contact with reality. This is precisely the havoc that sin has wrought within us, both by our own rebellion and by the distortion in others close to us.

Everyone has a damaged ego, because no one knows perfect love or is perfect. There is no such thing as a "superiority" complex. An air of superiority is an attempt to compensate for a deep sense of inferiority. It is but another mask we hide behind. If we all had a solid sense of our own dignity and worth, we would not be driven to act in a superior manner, but we would be free to express genuine humility. Much of what passes for humility is a subtle form of pride, rising from this distorted picture we have of ourselves. Underrating ourselves in the presence of others may be pride's way of fishing for a compliment. The way to find out what someone is really saying is to agree with him the next time he says something negative about himself. We would have to be naive about human nature not to know how that would turn out. Only a person with dignity can be truly humble.

Jesus Christ had a healthy self-esteem. He was the most self-asserting man history has ever known. He was certain of His own identity and He declared that identity. Any man who would claim that "before Abraham was I am,"[8] or identify Himself as the God who spoke to Moses as the "I am that I am,"[9] is very self-assured. But He was not self-centered. The thrust of His whole life was other-centeredness. There is a world of difference in being certain of one's identity and avowing that identity, and being self-centered.

A perfect illustration of this other-centeredness was given to us when Jesus washed the disciples' feet. It took place at the Last Supper, the night before His crucifixion. The disciples were in the midst of a power struggle: "And there was also a strife among them, which of them should be accounted the greatest."[10] Very typical and very human. In the midst of such crisis and agony for Christ, they were competing with each other for the number-one place. If ever there was a time for Christ to quit, this was it. He had labored for almost three years to change this egotistical attitude in His disciples. They had never seen it in Him. He had loved them and had patiently waited on them. He sought to pour Himself into them. From a human perspective, it looked hopeless. Here were the very men who had been touched by the greatness of God competing and trying to get ahead of each other. But Christ does not scold them, nor does He preach to them. In love, He stoops to serve them again. The Scripture says, "Jesus knew that the Father had put all things under his power, and that he had come from God and was returning to God, so he got up from the meal, took off his outer clothing, and wrapped a towel around his waist. After that, he poured water into a basin and began to wash his disciples' feet, drying them with the towel that was wrapped around him."[11] Knowing "that he had come from God, and was returning to God"—there was no question in His mind about His own identity. He knew who He was! His security and dignity rested with the Father. Before He could be destroyed, the Father would have to be destroyed. From this position of genuine dignity, He was free to turn all of His energies outward to serve those men. He could stoop, in humility, to wash the disciples' feet. He was doing for them what they could not do for themselves. With their competitive spirit, not one of them could have gotten over his own wall of pride to serve the others. Christ became for them what He purposed them to be for others—servants.

Only a person with a solid sense of his own dignity can have genuine humility, and be free to pour himself out in the service of others. Otherwise, we must reserve our energies to keep up our pretense of importance. Much of our energy is often spent trying to convince ourselves and others that we are significant, because deep down we fear that we are not. This keeps our attention upon ourselves, which is always destructive. With a proper love of self, we can focus our attention upon those around us and seek to understand them and to meet their needs. This is the secret of truly great people. The person who knows he is important need not work at proving his importance. He can serve others, irrespective of whether they recognize his worth or not. Every person is important, but no person is all-important. The real thing is to be a person of worth in Christ, and not simply give that impression.

There is another reason why we need a proper love of self. We give other people the same consideration we give ourselves. If I have trouble liking and accepting myself, I will have trouble liking and accepting other people. If I think of myself as a phony, I will think of others as phonies. If I am hard on myself, I will be hard on others. Now, the need to be accepted and liked by other people may keep me from expressing my attitude toward them, but it exists within me just the same. These unexpressed feelings become a tremendous source of resentment and hostility. I have noticed that I have the most trouble with my wife and others closest to me when I am having the most trouble with myself. The closer we come to a realistic concept of ourselves and a proper love of self, the more rewarding our relationships with others will become.

In a conference one of the participants responded to a discussion on proper love of self my saying, "I don't understand. My problem is that I love myself too much." It is difficult to communicate at this point, because of semantics. We hear each other according to our own particular thought patterns, and it is difficult to articulate in a different way. But I feel this is such an essential biblical and psychological insight for personal maturity that it is worth struggling with. It is true that most of us have an ocean full of self-love. We are loving the self that can only care for its own welfare and for those who contribute to its welfare. This element in us turns life into selfish exploitation. To love and nurture this self-centered self is destructive for everyone involved. This self must be crucified every time it shows its ugly head.

One man said, "That sounds like you are dividing man up again." The truth of the matter is that sin has divided man against himself. From this inner division comes a fragmentation of life, so that few people are ever able to do anything whole-heartedly. This inner strife dissipates a person's energies, so that it is almost impossible to pursue a goal with the intensity of one's whole personality. But if a person's imagination could be captured by the "image of God" potential within and by the "person he will be in Christ" concept, so that his whole life flows out in that direction, then a proper love of self would emerge. This would be the exact opposite of self-centeredness. It was this proper love of self that enabled Paul to write to the church at Philippi, without pride, "Whatever you have learned or received or heard from me, or seen in me—put it into practice. And the God of peace will be with you."[12] The people who had heard and seen Paul took this, not as an egotistical man saying, "Look at me!" but as one who had been so captured by Christ that, even in the midst of his own mistakes, men saw God in him.

The "image of God" potential is composed of the inner resources and possibilities that we have because we are made in God's image. One man gave an interesting formula for human personality. I feel it expresses something of the potential within. He said, "Personality equals Native Abilities multiplied by Inner Attitudes equaling Infinitude (Inexhaustibility)." Something has to happen on the inside of a person to release the inherent potential. It's like working with a small piece of uranium. We could beat that rock into dust and nothing would happen. We could melt it, and still nothing would happen. We could blow it up, but nothing would happen, except to change its shape. But if we did something to the nucleus within, a small piece fully released would blow New York City from the face of the earth. People are like that. We can push each other around, trying to force something productive to happen, with little result. We can threaten each other and manipulate each other, and we may get a few changes. But let God-in-Christ have the right of way within a person's life, and that person becomes a new creature. The potential within begins to be released, and the results are marvelous to behold.

A girl in her late teens was brought to me for counseling. She was very rebellious, and expressed her hostilities toward everyone around her. She resented being brought to me. The first few times we talked, we didn't accomplish much. Finally, I asked her why she disliked herself so much. The idea had never occurred to her. She felt everyone else was a slob, but she hadn't consciously focused on the picture she had of herself—which was pretty poor. We began to talk about what it means to be a person, and of the hidden, unexpressed potential within. I tried to assure her that I saw her as a person of worth, and she responded to my assurances of acceptance. As a result, she began a spiritual pilgrimage with Christ, and the change that took place in her was so remarkable that her parents could scarcely believe it. She has since become a teacher and has been ministering in a slum area, helping children in their studies.

That is what Christ comes to do—to free us to real personhood and to enable us to give away what He is giving us! But, a person with a poor self-image has little to give.

In summary, the two great commandments are, "to love God with one's whole being and to love one's neighbor as one's self." We do not begin, in the strictest sense, at the point of giving God love. We begin by responding to God's love in faith. We cannot really begin to give our neighbors—those life puts next to us—love until we have a genuine sense of proper self-love. Have you ever tried to love the unlovely?

A quality greater than any naturally within us has to enter our hearts before we have the capacity to give love to the unlovely. The beginning place is with one's self.

For several years, I lived with the realization that God loved me—but I was not sure He liked me, because I didn't like myself. One day I asked myself, "What does God's love purpose to do in me?" In seeking the answer, I found that He wants to conform me to the image of His Son.[13] I also found that He purposes to demonstrate in the ages to come "the incomparable riches of his grace, expressed in his kindness to us in Christ Jesus,[14] and that "when he appears, we shall be like him."[15] I found that I could love openly and unashamedly the man I am becoming in Christ. This gave me a new kind of self-acceptance and a patience with myself that I had never had before. All of a sudden, I could relax on the inside. I was His person, and He was doing something in me in which I could trust and rejoice. Then the strangest thing happened. I looked at the people around me and saw for the first time this same potential in them. I wanted somehow to communicate this to them. I didn't want to do anything that would keep them from knowing who they were and what God had in store for them. I began to realize that probably for the first time in my life, I was beginning to give God love.

> This is love: not that we loved God, but that he loved us and sent his Son as an atoning sacrifice for our sins. Dear friends, since God so loved us, we also ought to love one another. No one has ever seen God; but if we love each other, God lives in us and his love is made complete in us. We know that we live in him and he in us, because he has given us of his Spirit . . . If anyone says, "I love God," yet hates his brother, he is a liar. For anyone who does not love his brother, whom he has seen, cannot love God, whom he has not seen. And he has given us this command: Whoever loves God must also love his brother.[16]

As I opened up to God's love and began to find out what His love purposed to do in me, I began to taste what I have called "proper self-love." This began without conscious effort, to spill over in my attitudes toward others and my relationships with them. This became for me the first objective evidence that perhaps I was beginning to give God love. I have only tasted this, but the taste is good!

The change in attitude and perspective that comes with proper self-love is great! We can begin to rejoice in other's accomplishments, because we know we all count in God's economy. We begin to sense kinship with all humanity, and become enriched by what God is doing in others.

Christ has come to restore the potential for good in human beings that sin has distorted. That is "good news" indeed.

QUESTIONS

1. What four words would you use to describe yourself? Which one best describes you?
2. Are you more like your father or your mother?
3. Do inside or outside forces cause most of your trouble?
4. Name two qualities you like about yourself. Two you dislike.
5. Do you have a positive or negative self-image? Who and what has contributed to the image you have of yourself.?
6. Are you aware of any feeling of inferiority?
7. What does the author mean when he says, "Jesus Christ had a healthy egoism"? Is there a difference in self-assertion and self-centeredness? Can you recognize the difference in yourself?
8. How can we change our image?
9. How does the Christian faith wed dignity and humility?
10. Why do we fail so miserably at times?
11. How can we help others become whole persons?
12. Do you rejoice in the successes of others?
13. Are you still trying to prove yourself?
14. Do you believe God really likes you?
15. Can you recognize your feelings toward others as being

in character with the way you really feel toward yourself?
16. Can you see why *affirmation* heals and *condemnation* crushes?
17. How do you respond to affirmation?
18. Does it bother you to lose? Why?
19. Is it hard for you to show emotion? Why?
20. Is it hard or easy for you to accept help? Why?
21. What do you enjoy doing the most?
22. Are you easily liked?
23. Do you enjoy your own company?
24. Is there any part of your body that you would change?
25. Is it hard to admit you are wrong or to say "I am sorry"?
26. Do you usually finish what you start?
27. Are you easily hurt?
28. How do you handle conflict?

CHAPTER 6

GOD'S MAGNIFICENT OBSESSION

For God has allowed us to know the secret of His plan . . . that in all which will one day belong to (Christ) we have been promised a share.

Every person needs a perspective of life that is comprehensive enough to give meaning to all of existence, especially his own. Yet whether our perspective is comprehensive enough or not we all have presuppositions which rest upon that which we consider to be the truth of what exists. Everything we experience is interpreted and dealt with on the basis of our world view.

Roger Shinn, in his book *Christianity and the Problem of History,* says, "The question of life's meaning lies in the background of most serious thought and imagination, whether of primitive peoples or of the great speculative philosophers. To cease to ask the question may be the mark, not of keenness but of emptiness."[1]

We must be motivated to reach beyond ourselves or life has no purpose. To live for the moment is to retreat to the animalistic level of existence. This can be illustrated by considering one's goals in life. When someone reaches a goal that has been desired and pursued, and no other goal to reach for in the future exists, frustration will result. His energies and abilities are without direction until he finds another objective. It is said of Alexander the Great that he wept because there were no more worlds to conquer; he had achieved his goal, and he was without challenge and purpose. The writer of Proverbs says, "Where there is no vision, the people perish."[2]

Being finite human beings, if our world view is shaped only by human speculation and reason, then every thinking person must live with tremendous anxiety. How can we, with our finite resources, ever hope to have any certainty about the validity of our world view?

The Christian has the advantage when it comes to finding a comprehensive perspective of life. He is not left to speculation, or to his own reason. The Christian viewpoint is based on revelation, which is God's initiative in revealing Himself and His purposes to men. This revelation reaches its ultimate in Jesus of Nazareth, the God-Man; and it includes His birth, life, death, resurrection, ascension, return, and His eternal Lordship. It is the Christ-Event that furnishes the key for understanding the meaning of history and the goal of creation. He is the One who came from God, who was God and who reveals to all mankind the mind and the heart and the will of God.

To understand and to articulate this "open secret" becomes an exciting and expanding task. In an attempt to state the meaning and purpose revealed in Christ, we must remember that God is always greater than our concept of Him, and His purposes are far beyond our ability to comprehend. This does not mean that some understanding and comprehension cannot be reached, but it does mean that we must accept the reality of having incomplete knowledge. Eternity will be an unfolding, learning experience. We will never know all. But we can know enough to participate in God's eternal purpose and be captivated and enthralled by the revelation He has given us!

For years after making my beginning with Christ, I had no real understanding of what God was purposing in Christ. Even after I entered the ministry, the best I could do was to present the Gospel piecemeal. I recognized that Christ was the answer to man's dilemma. I saw escape from destruction, and heaven beyond death in Him. And I knew that in Christ I had a new life and a new beginning. There was no question that I needed to be related to Him "by grace through faith," but beyond that I could only exhort people to pray, to read the Scriptures, to participate in church life and to be moral. Though there was some validity in this approach, I had little understanding of the greatness of the new life that He came to give me, or of the transforming power of grace and faith. There was not much cohesion in the messages I presented—just a vast variety of emphases. I have since learned that life needs to be lived—not merely by punctuating it with a series of exclamation points—but with a sense of being caught up in a great purpose with meaning and destiny in it.

We were made to give ourselves to something. This is evidenced especially among youth. Give them disjointed information and there will be little response. Give them a purpose, a cause, a challenge and they respond wholeheartedly. Information increases knowledge, but the pursuit of an exciting objective produces enthusiasm. The message of Christ presents an exciting objective, but that message needs to be seen as a message of life, and not a preachment of morality.

In a study dealing with the "Priesthood of Christ" I saw something that overwhelmed me. I sat and wept like a child. I saw that I had taken something as magnificent as the Gospel of Christ and had so muddled it up and watered it down, that it could not awaken in me, or in the people to whom I ministered, a sense of greatness. Something stirred within me. With all my heart I wanted to participate in God's redemptive purpose as I was beginning to see it with new eyes. I could not wait to get back to my church to share with our people this "good news." My preaching changed immediately. No longer was I straining to find something to preach. I had so much to share that my problem changed from "what to preach" to "where to start." I had a new perspective—not new to the Scriptures, but new to me. What God was doing in Christ was so great that I had to share it. I was intoxicated by the message of Christ!

Twenty years have passed and I have not completely sobered up yet. "God's purpose in Christ" has become my song, which lifts me higher every time I sing it. It was in the Scriptures all the time, but I had not seen it. I have gossiped this "good news" on every occasion that has since presented itself.

How can I share on paper, in a brief but meaningful way, the message that has captivated me for these past twenty years? Whatever I write will be far short of the greatness of God's purpose. I must begin by suggesting that you read Ephesians and Colossians, in at least two different translations, keeping this question in mind: "What has God undertaken in Christ?" Paul has, under the direction of the Holy Spirit, comprehended something of the magnitude of what Christianity means to God. My effort here will be to present in a popular style what I understand the purpose of God-in-Christ to be.

If creation is an expression of God's purpose, then it bears witness to something stupendous in the making. Warren C. Young, in his book, *A Christian Approach to Philosophy*, illustrates the vastness of creation:

> Suppose that man were able to perfect a space ship which would travel at the speed of light itself (186,000 miles per second). At that speed he could travel the distance from the earth to the sun in about eight minutes. It would take him about four and a half hours to reach Neptune. Traveling at the same rate of speed it would occupy Captain Video for about 50,000 years to travel through our own galaxy! . . . Still traveling at the speed of light he would arrive at our nearest galactic neighbor in about a million years; or should he wish he might continue his journey to other galaxies whose distance from

us has been estimated at two to six billion light years![3]

It has been estimated that there are more than one hundred million such galaxies, and the end is not yet. Once when I used this illustration, I was asked, "What does that do to your concept of God?" I replied, "It just means that God is bigger than I thought!" When God creates a universe, He does it as God would do it! There is ample room for His purposes to be expressed. Yet God's purpose in Christ for man is so great that it will take two worlds for it to be completely unfolded. It will take both the finite and the infinite, this world and the world to come, for it to be fully expressed.

I choose to call this purpose "God's magnificent obsession." In Hebrews 12:2 the writer challenges us to "fix our eyes on Jesus, the Pioneer and Perfector of our faith, who for the joy set before him endured the cross, scorning its shame, and sat down at the right hand of the throne of God." (NIV) The mission of Christ was not drudgery. It was the *joy* that was set before Him that enabled Him gladly to endure a cross. Whatever thrills the mind and heart of God will be something for us to take seriously. It will be great enough to stagger our imagination. His purpose, which is an expression of His own character and love, will cause every knee to bow and every tongue to "confess that Jesus Christ is Lord, to the glory of God the Father."[4] The devil will not like it, but even he will have to take his hat off to a purpose and a love so great.

As I have already indicated, the meaning of creation cannot be found in the universe itself, but in Christ. Paul says,

> It is through him, at the cost of his own blood, that we are redeemed, freely forgiven through that full and generous grace which has overflowed into our lives and opened our eyes to the truth. For God has allowed us to know the secret of his plan, and

it is this: he purposes in his sovereign will that all human history shall be consummated in Christ, that everything that exists in Heaven or earth shall find its perfection and fulfillment in him. And here is the staggering thing—that in all which will one day belong to him we have been promised a share (since we were long ago destined for this by the one who achieves his purposes by his sovereign will), so that we as the first to put our confidence in Christ, may bring praise to his glory![5]

Sin caused a great rift in all of creation. Christ bridges the chasm created by sin to re-unify the Creator and the created. For man, the Incarnation of Christ is the eternal union of God and man. It becomes God's firm grip upon humanity, so that through the believer's unity with Christ, he may be lifted to share in the life of God as a son. This is not a pantheistic reabsorption into Deity. It is the creation of a "new humanity in Christ," which becomes the center of God's effort and purpose, and constitutes the ultimate exercise of His power. At great expense to God these "new men in Christ" are being brought by grace to possess a quality of life that is inexhaustible and to share in the kind of unity found in the Godhead. The vivid distinction between Creator and created remains. As one person expressed it, "This is to stand next to God, but not to be God."

This must be the most daring concept that has crossed the mind of man—that the God who fashioned this vast universe would reach out to an insignificant, self-centered person like me and offer to share His life with me. It's beyond my comprehension! Peter says it this way: "It is through him that God's greatest and most precious promises have become available to us men, making it possible for you to escape the inevitable disintegration that lust produces in the world and to share in God's essential nature."[6] He could give us a universe to rule over, and it would be nothing compared to allowing us to share in His life as His children.

We begin to share in the life God offers the moment we receive Jesus as our Savior and Lord. But full maturity in this life awaits us in the life to come. For the believer, the best is always yet to be. The devil gives us the best he has initially—then disillusionment follows. The Lord has much to give to His children, but He apportions His good gifts only as we are able to receive them.

The resurrected Christ gives us this beautiful invitation to share His life: "Here I am! I stand at the door, and knock. If anyone hears my voice and opens the door, I will come in and eat with him, and he with me."[7] Christ takes the initiative. He seeks us. If we recognize Him and allow Him to come into our experience, He offers to sit at our table and share our meal. He will eat what we eat. He will participate in our ups and downs, in our failures and successes, in our tragedies and triumphs. He offers to go with us through all that comes our way. And, that's not all! He invites us to eat what He has to eat; to participate in His life and in His strength; to share in His ability to deliver the goods; and to draw from His power to overcome evil and to accomplish the Father's will. To be asked to participate in life with God Himself is the greatest of all invitations.

This "new race" is destined to be conformed to the image of the resurrected Christ. No one is capable of becoming a little Christ, because in Christ the potential of the whole human race is expressed in its fullest sense, but we are becoming like Him in character and life. What a destiny to have! God is not exploiting us, but is bringing us to genuine fulfillment and wholeness. Our own uniqueness is being preserved and brought to its fruition in Him. Our personal identity becomes more distinct. Yet we shall share, through our unity with Him, in the rich variety of all of God's people plus richness of the life of God Himself. This is one reason that heaven cannot be a static place. Each person will have the richness of his own uniqueness to give to others, and he in turn will share in the abundance of the diversity of all the other. This means each will have more to give and each will give to his fullest. The possibilities that come from this kind of relationship approach infinitude, with something new and fresh to experience continually. Hell will have an abundance of boredom, but heaven will be unbelievably exciting.

These "new men" in Christ will be the sons through whom God will express His unconditional love and pour out His inexhaustible riches—both in this world and in the world to come. They are to be the means through which God expresses Himself in history. The believers are to be "the salt of the earth . . . and the light of the world."[8] They are to be the problem-solvers and the pattern-setters. They are in the world, but not of the world. Christ prays for His disciples: "My prayer is not that you take them out of the world but that you protect them from the evil one. They are not of the world, even as I am not of it . . . As you sent me into the world, I have sent them into the world."[9] God purposes to love His world through His people, as He loved it through His Son. This means that the believer is not being saved out of the world to a reserved place of happiness in heaven, but is being caught up in the life of God, which manifests itself best in servanthood.

God's people are to become His servants to His world. This will have a distinct effect upon the way the believer looks at the present world. This world, with its puzzling mixture of sorrows and joys, defeats and sucesses, becomes the arena for expressing the life within and for cutting out character, which is eternal. There is continuity between this life and the life to come. When I die, I am not going to cease to be Creath Davis and become some "Holy Joe." I will begin with what I end with here, except that all traces of sin will have been removed, and I will be capable of understanding even as I have been understood. So the way I respond to life and to God today has eternal consequences. I dare not waste life! I am living for and in eternity now. Christ, through the Holy Spirit, gives adequate resources to the believer for facing all of life with intensity, and for making this world the object of his growing powers of redemptive love and energy.

The believer also sees history moving toward a climax

and a conclusion. History is moving in a spiral toward a consummation. It is not simply repeating itself—it has a purposeful direction. History will conclude with the Second Coming of Christ, which will also usher in the infinite phase of God's redemptive purpose. The Second Coming of Christ is not just a dread day of retribution; it guarantees the ultimate victory of the Christian enterprise. This can give man hope, and can help him labor faithfully in the face of seeming defeat. He knows his work is not in vain in the Lord. It is hard to make a man give up when he knows that, ultimately, he will win.

In the world to come, this "new race," in its unity with and its conformity to the resurrected Christ, will possess a life of endless growth, experiencing an unfolding of the never-ending qualities and achievements inherent in the inexhaustible Being of God. This "Family of God" will be the medium, the voice, the creative hands by which God will do even greater things than the making of the cosmic universe.

In the first two chapters of Ephesians Paul describes our destiny in Christ. Once we have committed our life to Jesus Christ with an irrevocable commitment to being conformed to His image at any cost, He will accomplish in us all He purposes. Only His grace can enable us to come to such full commitment. He commits Himself to us, to one day bring us to the place that God Himself will say, "I am rich to have you as my son." When He finishes His work in us, I imagine that He might set us on a pedestal—right in the midst of heaven—and call all the great Beings to come and see what He has made. There we will be on exhibition—naked, with every molecule of our person and character exposed. God will turn us around and around for all to see. (When I was using this illustration on one occasion, a fellow broke in and said, "You had me about convinced that that's where I wanted to go until you told me that." But he had not allowed me to finish.) The kind of person we will be in Christ will be so amazing that all the angels will say, "Oh, Jehovah, we saw You when You created the universe and the world and the beauty of it, but we've never seen anything like what You have done in that sinner." And God Himself will say, "Son, you cost me dearly; but I am rich in what you have become. Now, jump down from there, we've got work to do—together."

In his prayer in Ephesians 1, Paul declares "how gloriously rich God's portion in His people is."[10]

We shall teach the angels! Peter, speaking of God's salvation in men, says, "which things the angels desire to look into."[11] In the ages to come God is going to demonstrate "the exceeding riches of His grace in His kindness toward us through Christ."[12]

Everyone, I guess, has some secret dream of what he wants heaven to be like. But whatever God has intended us to be and to do will stagger the imagination. Let your imagination run wild and dream as big as you can, and still it will be far short of what God has actually planned. Paul says, "No eye has seen, no ear has heard, no mind has conceived what God has prepared for those who love him."[13]

No one knows what we will do in heaven, but we can know something of the kind of people we will be. Here is an illustration I heard that portrays the character and ability we will possess: One day the Lord might call us up and say, "Son, I have a universe a few million light years away that is in trouble, and I want you to go straighten it out." We won't say, "Who me?" or "How?" We will be the kind of people who will already have adequate resources within for such a demanding task. And that task just might be to experience an incarnation and to pour out our life on behalf of that world. But, we will be so other-centered in character, that we will accept the task eagerly—grateful to serve!

I have never been disappointed in the "good news" of Christ when I have understood it. I continue to be delightfully surprised to find that what God has undertaken in Christ is so much more than I expected.

In the twelfth chapter of Romans, the first two verses, Paul insists that, in the light of the greatness of God's action, there is but one conclusion to which our reason can bring us—that is to give ourselves as servants through whom God can express His purpose.

QUESTIONS

1. What excites you most about life? What gives you a sense of meaning and purpose?
2. Have you ever consciously thought about the meaning you have for your own life as it relates to the meaning and purpose of history and eternity?
3. How can we find God's purpose for history and eternity from the Christian perspective?
4. If creation is a partial expression of God's creative purpose, what does creation communicate about that purpose?
5. If you really believed that God was sharing His life with you, what would be your response? What effect would it have on your *hopes* and *fears*? On your feelings about yourself and others? About the future?
6. Can you see how being caught up in a purpose as great as what God has revealed in Christ would eliminate dullness and boredom, and would create a continuing sense of excitement and direction?
7. Are you a planner and a goal setter? What goals have you or would you like to set for yourself to achieve over the next year? Over the next three years?
8. How would you like to be remembered when you die?

CHAPTER 7

ISOLATION IS INSANITY

For none of us can live alone by himself, and none of us can die alone by himself; indeed, if we live, we always live in relation to the Lord, and if we die we always die in relation to the Lord. So whether we live or die we belong to the Lord.

Life was never meant to be a solitary existence. To be totally cut off emotionally from personal relationships would produce insanity. A person could be isolated physically for a long period of time without becoming insane if there had been a meaningful relationship with someone in his past— someone who had awakened genuine selfhood in him. To know and be known by someone awakens something within us that sustains us. Dr. Bernard Steinzor, in his book, *The Healing Partnership*, says, "The person who appears completely alone may be a hermit in the wilds of the woods, but he is in communion with memories, nature and his God."[1] But, someone who is emotionally isolated, though physically in the midst of a multitude, is in a psychotic condition. Again Dr. Steinzor says, "The person who feels completely alone and has lost hope of a relationship will become a patient in the back wards of the mental hospital or a suicide."[2]

If an infant could be physically cared for without any kind of human relationship, he would be less than human. His personality would never develop, and he would act much as an animal. We pass on our humanity, good or bad, through relationships. It is through associating with others that our culture, knowledge, and history are transmitted. We are always just one generation away from regressing to barbarism. Our relationships furnish the necessary orientation to life so that every culture may progress.

Masculine and feminine roles are learned through relationships. They are learned first by copying mother or father. Both mother and father play significant and much needed roles in the child's life. A little boy needs a masculine image which only a man can supply. A little girl needs a feminine image which only a woman can supply. But, in the teens, it is the mother who communicates to her son what it means to be a man by the way she relates to him, and the father helps the daughter to know what it means to be a woman by his relationship to her. The alliance that allows the most complete discovery of what it means to be male or female is marriage.

If you have ever moved from your home town, you have felt the pangs of being separated from those you know and love, and of being thrust among strangers. Your relationships with people do more toward making you feel comfortable than your physical surroundings. You never feel at home until you are at home with someone. I grew up in a rural area, and I loved the woods and fields. When I visited the city, I always came away determined never to live in a metropolitan area. Everything seemed so crowded and noisy. Today I live in the city, and feel very much at home. I still miss the countryside, but the relationships I have established here make this city "home."

Man was made for meaningful relationships. In the Genesis account, man was made in the image of God to have dominion over the rest of creation, and to share in an uninhibited relationship with God. It was in the cool of the day, when evidently God was accustomed to dialoguing with Adam, that Adam hid from God because he had disobeyed. Sin had broken his perfect union with God. The rest of the Bible is the record of God's initiative in seeking to redeem this fallen creature, and to reestablish a loving, trusting relationship.

Not only was man to have a meaningful relationship with his Creator, who was above him, but also with his peers, beside him. The first bond of union was marriage:

> The Lord God said, "It is not good for the man to be alone: I will make a helper suitable for him . . . So the Lord God caused the man to fall into a deep sleep; and while he was sleeping, he took one of the man's ribs and closed up the place with flesh. Then the Lord God made a woman from the rib he had taken out of the man, and he brought her to the man. The man said, "This is now bone of my bones and flesh of my flesh; she shall be called 'woman,' for she was taken out of man." For this reason a man will leave his father and mother and be united to his wife, and they will become one flesh.[3]

Marriage becomes the training ground for relating to another in love and openness, and furnishes the opportunity for achieving unity.

Relationships are so important that Buber, in his book, *I and Thou*, says, "All real living is meeting"[4] — God and others! "The lesson of human development is that from birth to death man is always becoming a complexity of relationships. The self is a more or less fluid patterning of relationships whose change or permanence depends on the stability of the relationship of which the person is a part."[5] The measure of life is the quality of our personal relationships. A person is only as rich or as poor as the quality of his relationships.

A popular university student who became president of the student body his senior year said that he could call a large percentage of the students by their first names, but, he realized later, he hadn't really come to know any student well. His own evaluation of his university experience was that four years of his life were impoverished, because his friendships were only superficial. A person who in a loving, trusting relationship knows and is known by one other human being is rich indeed, and he need not fear being open to the world. It is the person who has never been open with another who most fears being exposed. Sidney Jourard says, "Every maladjusted person is a person who has not made himself known to another human being and in consequence does not know himself. Nor can he be himself. More than that, *he struggles actively to avoid becoming known by another human being.* He works at it ceaselessly, 24 hours daily; and it is work!"[6]

One man said to me, "You have to be careful in your relationships with other people. It's dangerous to get to know someone too well, because you know 'familiarity breeds contempt.' " This is true, if it is familiarity between two masks. If two people attempt to know one another, yet neither is willing to lay aside his disguise, the relationship has to be fraudulent. The natural result of such an unrealistic relationship is contempt. The Bible calls it "hypocrisy," and hypocrisy is tragic because it isolates a man from others and short-circuits life. But the meeting of real persons is the most stimulating and creative kind of experience that human beings can have.

Martin Buber has delineated two kinds of relationships—the I-Thou and the I-It.[7] The I-Thou relationship is the most basic. Out of it persons emerge as persons. In the I-Thou relationship both the I and the Thou are affected. Each has a sense of his own worth as a person and values the other as well. This relationship is based upon the ability of one person to enter and share deeply the life of another, without losing his own identity or individuality. Not only does he share in the rich variety of another's personality, but in the relationship he exercises the aptitudes which make him more strikingly unique. The hidden, unexpressed qualities within each are released, and the relationship becomes richer and even more creative.

Dr. Paul Tournier shared out of his own pilgrimage toward selfhood, in a conference at Laity Lodge, something that illustrates the power of the person-to-person relationship. His parents died when he was young and he went to live with an aunt and uncle. His aunt was mentally ill. Dr. Tournier related how, as a result, he grew up not knowing how to relate to people. He was locked inside himself. In school a Greek professor took an interest in him, and often invited young Paul home with him to sit in front of the fireplace and visit. Paul's relationship with the professor broke the bonds of his repressed inner self. He was released from being a retiring, restricted lad and became a brilliant student and a leader of a national youth movement in Switzerland.

The power of the I-Thou relationship is fantastic. Dr. Tournier was awakened to genuine personhood by it. But, in an I-Thou relationship the results are never one-way— both persons are affected. Dr. Tournier said that when he, as a young Christian medical doctor, wrote the manuscript for his first book, the one evaluation of it that he wanted most was that of his Greek professor. So he made an appointment with the professor and went to his home. He read his first chapter with a great deal of anxiety as the old professor listened. After he finished, there was complete silence. Dr. Tournier awaited his opinion. After a few moments the professor said, "Paul, read on." He read another chapter. Again, silence. This procedure continued through the reading of the entire manuscript. After the last chapter, Dr. Tournier said the old professor looked at him and, "Paul, I feel that we need to pray together."

"But, Sir," Dr. Tournier queried, "I didn't know you were a Christian."

The professor replied calmly, "I am."

"But, since when?"

"As of this moment."

I was deeply moved as I heard Dr. Tournier relate this experience. The power of personal involvement is immense. It struck me how much we need to present our witness in the context of meaningful, authentic relationships, so we do not become peddlers of the Gospel.

The other relationship that Buber mentions is the I-It relationship: "Without *It* man cannot live. But he who lives with *It* alone is not man."[8] There is legitimate concern with things, using them as an expression of one's own life and creativity. The tragedy comes when we seek to relate to another person as an *It* instead of a *Thou*. To use another person as a prop for our own ego, or to manipulate him for our purposes is to relate to him as a *thing* and not as a person. This becomes a form of murder and suicide. In relating to human beings as things, we destroy them, and ourselves as well. An example of this is looking upon a woman only as an object of sex and never seeing her as a person. This makes her less than human, and destroys in the lustful observer his own capacity for a meaningful relationship with the opposite sex.

I am convinced, both from my own struggle toward genuine selfhood and from being involved with fellow strugglers, that the manner in which a person relates to God, to others, and to himself is a simple but accurate barometer of his life. I can understand myself best in terms of my relationships with others.

After discussing the need to be related, one man asked, "How can I relate to God? I can't see Him or touch Him, and I certainly don't want to believe in something that isn't there." None of us wants to believe in someone or something that isn't there, but there is a way we can know God and be related to Him, if we so desire. The way is not by the methods used in scientific investigation—God cannot be proven in a test tube. God can only be known in a personal way, through a relationship. This should not surprise us, because this is the only way we can know any person—by being involved with him.

In John 17, we have Christ's prayer in which He offers Himself, His work, and His people unto the Father. His work was to give eternal life to those the Father had given to Him. It was to be given as the by-product of a relationship.

"For you granted him authority over all people that he might give eternal life to all those you have given him. Now this is eternal life: that they may know you, the only true God, and Jesus Christ, whom you have sent."[9] This eternal life is not simply life prolonged indefinitely. It is life under new management—God's instead of mine—with an inexhaustible quality. Eternal life is such that the living of it produces its own dynamics and its own reward. Nothing need be added to it, because it never becomes dull or stagnant. There is always something new and exciting to experience in it. It is no cheap trip to heaven, but a participation in the God-kind of life. Christ never intended that we wait until we get to heaven to learn the nature of His kind of life. He said of His own mission, "I am come that they might have life, and that they might have it more abundantly."[10] He Himself experienced this abundant (eternal) life while He lived here in the flesh. And it was this quality of life that He longed for His followers to know. Some have interpreted the Christian message as nothing more than "pie in the sky, by and by," with this life really not mattering much; but the biblical message informs us that we are living in eternity now, and that we have available to us unlimited resources for making life a thrilling adventure with God *now*.

Eternal life comes in knowing God. The Greek word for knowing God is *gnosko*—to know by experience. The person who experiences God in a personal relationship possesses eternal life. There are, however, many barriers which may keep us from fully realizing this quality of life. Misunderstanding is one. To think that because God has entered our experience we will no longer struggle with the ills and problems that beset all men is to open ourselves to disillusionment, and perhaps despair. Actually, God-in-Christ, through the Holy Spirit, comes to *abide* in us. He operates within the bounds of our temperament and our mentality. He participates in our life, with our struggles and problems, in such a way that His strength undergirds us, and the character that is formed is ours. This is Love's way of redeeming and transforming men.

Another obstacle to knowing God is the problem of the masks again. We can put a mask on the face of God and never see the real God of life. Our concept of God, true or false, will play a major role in the depth of our commitment to Him, and will also determine the way we view the world, the processes of life, ourselves, and others. We cannot wholeheartedly abandon ourselves to a God we cannot love. We must keep in mind that a man becomes like the God he worships.

What are some of the masks with which we cover the face of God? A popular one is that of our own image. This is to make Him simply a big man, or an extension of ourselves. What we encounter in coming to God with this mask is nothing more than our own ego. We mistake our own voice for the voice of God. This is part of the reason why men do such ridiculous things in the name of God.

We can try to make God a stern judge who anxiously awaits our mistakes, so He can condemn us. Or we can make Him a bookkeeper who follows us around, writing down every bad thing and every good thing we do, so that He can tally up the books one day to see if we made it. These concepts may create fear or rejection of God in us, but they will never allow us to love Him.

We may make God an impersonal force which operates irrespective of any concern for us. This means there would be no personal God with whom we could be reconciled. Again, a man would be shut up to himself and his own limited resources.

Or we might try to make God a rich uncle who has never known agony or hardship. This suggests that we must respond by buttering Him up, so He will lavish His riches upon us.

Some people may make God an indulgent grandfather, who exercises love devoid of strength or discipline. From this view a man can do as he pleases, with few consequences, if any.

Perhaps the major misconception of our day is that God is the keeper of the church, concerned only with religious activities, and with little or no contact with everyday life.

Nothing could be further from the truth than these ridiculous concepts. If we want to know God and the power of His life, we must remove the masks we have imposed on Him and face the God revealed in Jesus Christ: "For in Christ all the fullness of the Deity lives in bodily form."[11] I suggest that you read the gospels with this question in mind: What is the picture of Jesus of Nazareth presented in these remarkable accounts? It is fantastic how for centuries these simple records have weathered the most critical investigation by both the friends and enemies of Christ. Read first for impression, not for detail. Don't hurry, but read slowly and allow what you read to soak in.

The writer of Hebrews says, "In the past God spoke to our forefathers through the prophets at many times and in various ways; but in these last days he has spoken to us by his Son. . . the exact representation of his being, sustaining all things by his powerful word."[12] Jesus of Nazareth is the one unique God-Man. He is not half-God and half-man. He is one whole personality, but in that one personality resides the Godhead *and* all the potential of the human race.

In Jesus of Nazareth God is both revealed and concealed at the same time. God is concealed in Christ's humanity, because if we were to face God in all His glory we could not resist Him. We would be as satellites in orbit, without the power of choice. The only way we could see God fully, and remain human would be to be made like Him in character. John declares for the believer, "How great is the love the Father has lavished on us, that we should be called children of God! And that is what we are! The reason the world does not know us is that it did not know him. Dear friends, now we are children of God, and what we will be has not yet been made known. But we know that when he appears, we shall be like him, for we shall see him as he is."[13]

God is also revealed in the humanity of Christ. There was something about Him that stirred men to the depth of their souls. He was as a whirlwind going across a wheat field. Men were never the same after they met Him. Some hated Him and wanted to kill Him, because He threatened their preconceived ideas about God and life. Others loved

Him and left all to follow Him. One of those who knew Him best declared the deepest conviction of his soul when he said of Him: "Thou art the Christ, the Son of the Living God."[14]

What was He like? Volumes have been written to answer this question, yet we are far from a complete answer. He is beyond describing. No one can capture completely in words the magnificence of His Person. The writer of John's gospel says at the conclusion of his interpretive portrait of Christ, "Jesus did many other things as well. If every one of them were written down, I suppose that even the whole world would not have room for the books that would be written."[16]

What better way could God reveal Himself than in specific human events? He became Man "and lived for awhile among us. We have seen his glory. The glory of the one and only Son who came from the Father, full of grace and truth."[17] In becoming Man, He allowed us to see what God was like in everyday human conditions. As he encountered suffering—He was moved by it and reached out to heal. As He encountered grief—He was so sensitive to the hurt felt by the two sisters of Lazarus that He wept with them, participating in their grief, giving them hope, and restoring Lazarus. As he encountered those broken by sin — He forgave the prostitute in Samaria, freed her and gave her a new life.

Jesus never met an unimportant person. He awakened ordinary men to greatness!

There was something so winsome and warm about Him that even the little children were attracted to Him.

He was open for the world to see. He was the same on the inside as on the outside. There was no facade, no masking of the real self.

Men who, because of self-interest, deliberately closed their eyes to the truth stirred His anger. He expressed tremendous moral indignation and anger when He saw little children mistreated, or the hypocrisy of some people, or the strong exploiting the weak. He loved the sinner, but He hated the sin.

In Christ we see the kind of suffering love that can take all the hate and evil men can cast on Him, and still be Love which stoops to pick up the pieces.

In Christ we see the kind of servanthood that can, in dignity, bend down to wash men's feet, that they might escape self-centeredness and have a chance at real life.

If God is like Jesus of Nazareth, then my heart can rest in Him!

Along with removing the masks we put on the face of God, we must remove any pretense of our own in approaching Him. We must come naked, withholding nothing. To come to God in ruthless self-honesty, baring our lives before Him, is to discover what it is to be a real person. He knows all about us anyway, and He still loves us; but only as we stand exposed before Him and experience His love, forgiveness and healing, can we believe that He really does care about us. We need to tell Him how we really feel and what we have been thinking, good or bad. In those "down" periods when we speak frankly of our feelings, (which may even be of resentment toward Him for allowing us to get so down), He does not blow us out of existence. He waits in love for our stubborn hearts to accept His love and be healed.

The bases for this relationship between God and man are the most creative dynamics in the world—grace and faith. To mix achievement of self-effort with grace and faith as the foundations of our relationship with God is to dilute the potency of God's work in us. We must remember that the Christian is made by God: "For we are God's workmanship, created in Christ Jesus to do good works."[18] We begin and continue as God's person because of what He did and is doing, and not because of our achievement or merit. "For it is by grace you have been saved, through faith—and this is not from yourselves: it is the gift of God—not by works, so that no one can boast."[19] In the semantics of our day, we might add that it is "costly" grace and "radical" faith that saves. Costly grace is the way love acts toward the unlovely—not to destroy but to transform. God is dealing with us according to our needs, and not according to our just deserts. That is costly both to God and to us! It is expensive for God to get mixed up with you and me: "He who did not spare his own Son, but gave him up for us all— how will he not also, along with him, graciously give us all things?"[20]

Not only did grace cost God His Son, but it will also cost me *me*. This kind of unconditional love, unconditional forgiveness, and unconditional acceptance woos from me the sovereignty of my own life. And the sovereignty of my own life is the last stronghold of sin. We may give up doing some wrong things without much struggle, but the last thing we surrender is ourselves. Yet only when Christ becomes our Master are we truly free to live.

The Scriptures declare, "Therefore, if anyone is in Christ, he is a new creation; the old has gone, the new has come! All this is from God, who reconciled us to himself through Christ and gave us the ministry of reconciliation: that God was reconciling the world to himself in Christ, not counting men's sins against them. And he has committed to us the message of reconciliation."[21] God has been reconciled to the world and He was in Christ seeking to reconcile the world unto Himself. God did not rebel against us. We rebelled against Him. His love and forgiveness have been constants; we were the ones who fled from His face. He has pursued us even to sending His own Son. And Christ surrenders Himself into our hands. The moral imperative from this kind of love is that we abandon ourselves to him. In this relationship, Christ is bound to us with fetters that cannot be broken.

It is like a young wife who, before children come into her home, has a great deal of freedom, but once a little one comes, her life is no longer her own. She lives every minute in the light of the needs of that infant. You could not pay a woman enough to be a real mother. Only love is an adequate motivation for all she must give. Christ lives today in the light of our needs. What love, what costly love, He has for us.

There are no barriers from God's side. What keeps us from God is our unwillingness to come to Him.

This brings us to our part in this relationship—that of coming to God. God has acted on our behalf; we must respond. He came, He gave, we must receive. This receiving is faith. Faith in the beginning is a simple commitment to a Person, and that Person is Jesus Christ. It is the entrance into a relationship of trust, in which Christ is allowed to transform us completely. As faith grows, it becomes the exercise of a love-affair between a person and God, and tremendous creativity is released. We are launched into such a great adventure that even the angels learn from it: "Even angels long to look into these things."[22]

The secret of spiritual growth is to allow our relationship with Christ to continue unobstructed. Christ spoke of Himself as the "vine" and the believers as the "branches" which could do nothing without abiding in Him.[23] If the life-sap in the vine is allowed to flow into the branches, the natural result will be fruit. If our relationship to Jesus Christ is kept open, warm and vital, so the life-sap in Him can flow into us, the result will be abundance.

A meaningful relationship with another human being can aid us greatly in coming to a significant relationship with God. And once we have a realistic relationship with God, we can freely begin to open ourselves to those that life has put next to us, in a transforming relationship with them.

In this day, when people are being crowded closer together physically, but seem to be pushed further apart emotionally, "the people of God" desperately need to recapture the spirit of *koinonia*, which the New Testament believers had. *Koinonia* is the Greek word which is usually translated in English as "fellowship." This is really an extension of the I-Thou relationship, emersed in deep concern, to a larger community of people. This community of believers has much in common. They share their common humanity; but more, they share their acknowledgment of personal rebellion against God and their reconciliation to God through Christ. They have, in fact, become the "Body of Christ" in the world. God purposes through this people, who have received Christ as Savior and Lord, to love His world the way He loved it in Christ.

The Christian life was never meant to be a "lone ranger" experience. To say we do not need anyone to help us in our Christian venture is to say we do not need God to help us. Part of His way of helping us is through fellowship with His people. To renounce the power of fellowship is to be impoverished.

It was in a fellowship group in my pastorate that I learned the power of *koinonia*. One middle-aged man—a railroad brakeman with a fourth-grade education—was released from his timidity and inferiority complex by the power of that fellowship. His parents had died when he was a child, and he had experienced an extremely difficult childhood. As a result, he was so timid that, once when he went into an employment office to apply for a job, he hadn't the courage to tell the secretary his name, and he had to walk out of the office—a dejected failure. That same man, in the openness and warmth of Christian fellowship, discovered who he was and who God was. And he found that he had something unique to give to others.

The transformation was so remarkable that one of our deacons said to me, "I've been a deacon forty-seven years, but I've never seen anyone change like that man." He had such a winsome effect on his co-workers that they kept him awake at night asking questions about what had happened to him. He didn't know any better than simply to share what he was experiencing. Later, he was invited to a nearby college to speak to a group of ministerial students. He was so free and open with the students that everyone had tears streaming down their cheeks when he finished. There was not one trace of timidity remaining in him! Love had cast out all fear. He had become the best communicator in our congregation—a real witness for Christ.

What those men in that fellowship group did for me cannot be overestimated. They helped me to lay aside my preacher-mask, and accept myself as a fellow-struggler. We met early on Sunday mornings for a time of personal sharing and prayer. I was often so touched by the power of God to change lives, families, and vocations in that group, that at times it was almost more than I could contain. I spent many of the Sunday school hours at home, literally weeping, because I was so full after our sharing time. On a couple of occasions I was so full of gratitude for what God was doing that instead of preaching I could only weep. Somehow the Lord got through those tears, and our entire congregation responded with a warmth and openness that we had never before experienced.

May God help us to recover the power of fellowship!

The surest way to keep from being related meaningfully with other people is to go out aggressively looking for "a relationship." Relax, and begin opening yourself slowly to those around you, focusing your attention upon them and their needs. Looking for a relationship that will help me learn to relate is, again, only using the other person. If we want a friend, we must offer ourself as a friend. If we want to be accepted and respected, then we must give acceptance and respect. If we want love, we must give love.

The following is a list of some essential elements for meaningful personal relationships.

1. Meaningful relationships require two persons who are mature enough to relate to each other on the basis of each being a person of worth and dignity.

2. Each person must have enough independence that he does not become unduly anxious when he has to stand alone.

3. Each person must have sufficient self-acceptance, so that he is not driven compulsively to try to use the other person as a prop to his own ego, or as a necessary tool for his own welfare.

4. Each is given the freedom to express his own uniqueness.

5. Each appreciates the other, and feels that he has something of value to give to him. There is present the ability

to give and receive freely, without the sense of debt-repayment.

6. Because each is accepted as a person, there is a sense of security that stems from the fact that his acceptance is not conditional or temporary.

7. Each is aware of his own uniqueness, which is worthy of expression, and he does not seek to deny this by trying to change himself to gain the approval of others.

8. The relationship itself becomes more important than the immediate pain or pleasure of the persons involved, and can be maintained, even at the cost of temporary discomforts.

9. The instrinsic quality for this kind of relationship is nothing less than love.

QUESTIONS

1. Outside your immediate family, who has had the greatest influence on you? What were they like and what did they do?
2. What is your most meaningful relationship at present?
3. Whose approval is most important to you? Why?
4. Have you covered the face of God with any masks?
5. How can we know and be known by another?
6. What is Jesus Christ like?
7. Do you recognize the need to be deeply related to others?
8. What are some roadblocks to relating meaningfully to others and how can they be overcome?
9. How would you describe a healthy relationship?
10. What experiences have helped you develop meaningful friendships?
11. How will you start in deepening your relationships?

CHAPTER 8

FOR BETTER OR WORSE

So God created man in his own image, in the image of God created he him; male and female created he them. And God blessed them.

For better or for worse is exactly what marriage is. Most marriages have both these elements present at some point along the way. In the fairy tales that were read to us as we were growing up, the problems came before marriage, and the story ended with the knight and princess marrying and living happily ever after. The picture of marriage became some happy, blissful state with no more problems to challenge or threaten. The truth of the matter is that this kind of blissful state would be boring in heaven or on earth. Life is not life without growth, and marriage is not marriage without struggle. Any two people who share life-space as intimately as husband and wife cannot avoid conflict, either openly or secretly behind the scenes. It can be either creative conflict which keeps pushing us beyond ourselves, or it can be destructive discord which separates us emotionally and personally. No other relationship in the world has the potential that marriage does for growth or for destruction. It is in this alliance that self-centeredness reaps its greatest reward.

No other human relationship has such resilience. One couple, dear friends of mine, experienced a shattering of their marriage. The wife was involved with another man. The husband almost went berserk when he discovered it. It looked as though that marriage would be hopelessy destroyed. At separate times, during a two-year period of struggle, both the wife and the husband came to a vital faith in Jesus Christ. Their new-found commitment gave them resources they had not formerly possessed for dealing with their alienation from each other. Six years have passed, and the recovery of that marriage is a souce of deep encouragement to me. Their relationship is deeper and their communication greater than it was before their crisis. In a retreat dealing with marriage, this couple ministered so profoundly to all of us out of their own marital experience that one couple who have, what we would consider, a solid marriage, remarked, "It would almost be worth going through such hell, if the end result would be the quality of relationship they have achieved."

Almost any marriage, regardless of the crisis, could be beautiful and fulfilling, if both the husband and the wife really desired it to be. Dr. Paul Tournier says,

> What really counts, then, is the working out together of marital happiness. It is a goal to strive after, not a privilege gained at the outset. And to work it out, the ability to understand each other is essential. So-called emotional incompatibility is a myth invented by jurists short of arguments in order to plead for divorce. It is likewise a common excuse people use in order to hide their own failings. I simply do not believe it exists. There are no emotional incompatibilities. There are misunderstandings and mistakes, however, which can be corrected where there is a willingness to do so.[1]

"Where there is a willingness to do so" is the first secret for a great marriage. Meaningful marriages do not just happen. They must be created, and re-created, through great effort on the part of both husband and wife. But this effort need not be dull or burdensome. It can be an adventure—an adventure of love and discovery!

In a marriage where love is freely given and freely received, there is no saturation point. There will always be something fresh, new and exciting entering into the relationship. This loving relationship allows each partner to discover and express his or her own uniqueness, and each is enriched by the fuller discovery of the other. There is nothing boring about this kind of life. A man is a fool to neglect his marriage and so impoverish himself and his wife. Likewise, the wife who takes her husband for granted is selling her marriage short. The truth is that our greatest achievement or our greatest failure in this life will occur within our own marriage. No one wins in the failures, and both gain in the successes.

Forgiveness is an essential ingredient in a successful marriage. In such a close, intimate relationship, we cannot but hurt each other. We say things we regret after our temper cools. To hold these things in one's mind without forgiving would be to engender such resentment and hostility that there could be no real sharing of life.

Next to God's gift of Himself to men is God's gift of marriage. Man is incomplete in himself and woman is incomplete in herself. Both need the other for their own fulfillment and to complement the other. Part of man's aloneness is overcome in this relationship, and the door is opened to community. A world without woman would be a world with only a competitive spirit. There would not be the possibility of complementary relationships. Each man would be alone, competing with every other man. But in the gift of woman to man, God made possible the development of society, so there could be sharing of life in a complementary way which enriches all concerned. In the Genesis account God says, "It is not good for the man to be alone."[2] God brought all the living creatures before Adam to be named, but for Adam there was not found a helper suitable for him. God wanted Adam to recognize this before He created Eve. The Lord caused a deep sleep to fall upon Adam, and He took one of his ribs to make Eve. As someone pointed out, this bone was taken from Adam's side. It was not taken from his head for the woman to rule over him, nor from his foot for the woman to be dominated. But from his side was the bone taken, for the woman was to stand as an equal beside the man. When this relationship gets out of proper balance, each life is lessened.

God purposed that the goal of this relationship would be the achievement of unity. "For this reason a man will leave his father and mother and be united to his wife, and they will become one flesh."[3] It is in this kind of unity that a man learns what it means to be a man, and a woman learns what it means to be a woman; and both share in the oneness of their interdependent roles.

Unity is one of the manifestations of the eternal, the God-kind of life. Its ultimate perfection is found in the Godhead. As applied to men, the wonder of unity is that it enables even the least to have a quality of life which is eternal and boundless. This relationship enables each to continue growing and expressing the hitherto unexpressed within. Marvelously, this process never exhausts itself—the best is always yet to come. Couples engaged in the reality of oneness will experience life that moves from one level of abundance to higher and higher levels, which never end. People who miss this may want to re-live the honeymoon stage of marriage, because that seemed to be the best. But, for the couples who learn how go give themselves to each other, the honeymoon will still have been great, but inadequate to the growing, continuing relationship they are experiencing. There will always be a sparkle and zest to this marriage! It will be like an oasis in a desert. The marriage that has unity will be as close to heaven as anything on earth.

A new partner is not the answer for a troubled marriage. The answer lies in a real desire, by one or both, for a redemptive marriage. Achieving this is never easy, regardless of whom you marry. In any marriage, self-exposure is essential to achieving unity. As long as we keep secret our deep feelings, it can never be a reality. As Dr. Tournier points out.

> The most frequent fault seems to me to be the lack of complete frankness. I see many couples. Behind their difficulties I always discover this lack of mutual openness, a loyal and total openness to one another without which there can be no real understanding. A couple who are courageous enough always to say everything will without a doubt go through many upsets. but they will be able to build an ever more successful marriage. On the other hand, all dissimulating becomes only the portent, and the way toward, failure.[4]

We can live under the same roof without knowing each other. There must be open communication of thoughts, feelings, and convictions. It takes courage to be this transparent with anyone, even those closest to us. If we feel that our marriage partner is not opening his or her deeper feelings to us, we should understand that communication at this depth cannot be forced. Instead, we should begin to be a patient and receptive listener. This is not a technique, but the sharing of life. Remember, it is possible to hide our true feelings both while talking and in silence. Verbalizing does not necessarily mean communication is taking place. Yet, for couples who have learned to give themselves to each other, a great deal of communication can take place in silence. However, talking together is essential for the lines of communication to remain open.

Often there is a conflict between a man's vocation and his home life. This is understandable. Marriage is usually more of a career for the woman. When the little girls were playing house, the little boys were off on some adventure. The girl dreamed of having a happy home, while the boy dreamed of changing the world, or of going to the moon. Most men, while in the pursuit of their career, picked up a wife along the way. Consequently, they may have more to learn about marriage than the wife. After the honeymoon, a man will be tempted sorely to become absorbed in his occupation, especially if it is rewarding. He needs to realize this and consciously seek to avoid such total preoccupation. The wife needs to understand also, and allow some time for adjustments to take place. If she nags her husband or tries to be too possessive, she will only drive him further away.

Both need to realize that it is essential to spend time together. But, more important than the amount of time, is how well that time is spent. Is each allowing the other to share in his world? Is real communication taking place—of feelings as well as experiences and ideas? To be practical, I would suggest that the man who has great demands placed upon his time, schedule a definite period to be with his family. This will not be wasted time, because he needs his family and they need him if life is to be complete. To the wife, I recommend that she make the most of the time she does have with her husband, and not spend those precious hours complaining about not having more time. If she makes their time together a pleasant interlude, the husband will, no doubt, try harder to arrange more time. We receive by giving!

The wife must also guard against becoming preoccupied with her children, a career outside the home or other social activities. She needs to give her attention to achieving unity with her husband.

God planned man's journey into this kind of relationship well, using the second greatest drive of human personality as the avenue to unity. The sex drive is second only to survival. Sex and survival cannot be separated by any distance. They are interrelated, because the survival of the human race depends upon procreation. But the sex drive in human beings is different from the sex instinct in animals. In the animal world sex is for procreation alone, and it is without emotional involvement. In human beings, the primary purpose of sex is to help a man and a woman, who have fallen in love and have committed themselves to each other in marriage, to achieve unity. Once this state is achieved, the stage is set for bringing children into the world and giving them a fair chance at life. Unity makes the nest secure enough for children.

Sex is not evil. It is one of God's richest gifts to His children. If it is the meeting of two persons in a responsible relationship of love, it becomes an expression of the most intimate kind of communication and shared life. Sex is physical, but it is much more. If it becomes simply physical, the law of diminishing returns operates, and before long the sex experience has reached its saturation point for that couple. There begins to be less and less satisfaction. It is at this point that perversion and promiscuity may enter in to destroy whatever relationship is left.

When the sex experience becomes an expression of responsive love, the law of progression operates and there need never be a point of saturation. The experience will not lose its power and attractiveness in this marriage, but will increasingly acquire more quality and will be a deep expression of intimate love. Genuine satisfaction can be experienced on this level, which can give the wife a sense of security, and the husband a sense of fidelity.

It is a strange and beautiful thing that the wife is the one who gives her husband a sense of his own fidelity, and the husband is the one who gives his wife a sense of her own security. To achieve the kind of relationship that cannot be reduplicated anywhere, with anyone else, is the greatest safeguard for fidelity within the marriage. We have to learn how to achieve this kind of relationship. No marriage starts with it.

To use sex simply to relieve tension, or as a casual experience of pleasure, is to rob it of its quality. Engaging in promiscuity progressively destroys one's capacity for real love. The commandment, "Thou shalt not commit adultery,"[5] is for our benefit. God is not withholding anything beneficial from us. He purposes that we safeguard our capacity for real love, so that we can have the richness and the quality that it can bring to life. Those who disregard this reality are the losers.

One young man, who engaged in seducing young girls in his high school and college days, said that he would sit up in his bed at night, disgusted with himself, and weep, wishing he could die. He wanted to quit, but he found that he was mastered by his passions. They had created a living hell for him, which only the grace of God is enabling him to handle.

Man's fallen nature leaves him open to irresponsible and illicit sexual relationships. Such experiences may seem exciting in the beginning, but the cheap thrill inevitably becomes too costly. In counseling with men and women who have engaged in extramarital relationships, I have never yet found one who encountered anything but heartache in the end.

Again and again I have heard a man or a woman who was having an affair confess, "I just don't love my wife (or husband) any more. I don't see any reason for going on with our marriage." I usually reply by asking if they think they can know their true feelings while being involved with someone else, who has taken their attention away from their marriage partner. (Love is quite different from lust. Love willingly assumes responsibility. Lust is only interested in the pleasure gained.) One woman who responded positively to this question did agree to break off her affair for a period of time to see if she had any feeling left for her husband. She found that she did, and they have, with some struggle, made an empty marriage come alive.

There is only one way that life will work. We may stubbornly plot a course contrary to what is right, thinking that we will be the exception, but there are no exceptions in this matter of loving. The law of the harvest is as sure as God is. If we seek to make our marriage what it should be, the harvest will be a depth of love that will enrich everyone involved. It will do more for our children than all the proper training we can give them. The climate of the home affects the children more than the conversation of the home. If we haphazardly plod through our marriage, the result will be tragic for everyone concerned. Yet, the motivation for pursuing the quality and depth possible in marriage should not be fear of what might happen if we do not. It should be a sense of excitement and anticipation of being caught up in the wonder of it all!

One couple, who had been married eighteen years and had what anyone would consider a good marriage, decided they wanted to explore this matter of quality in sex. Although they had a relationship in this area that had sufficed, both had gained the wrong concept of sex. They had seen it more as part of man's lower nature. Now they wanted to achieve the kind of relationship that they had come to feel God wanted them to have. They prayed together, asking God to enable them to attain the kind of unity that He purposed. Consequently, they entered into deeper communication and were able to give themselves more completely to each each other. The result was a new quality in their sexual relationship. The husband told me that they were enjoying each other's company so much that they found it extremely painful to be separated for any length of time. He is a traveling salesman, and has started making as many of his calls as possible by phone. To see a couple, who have been married for almost twenty years, so wrapped up in each other, hardly able to wait to share their experiences and feelings together at the end of the day, presents a hopeful picture of marriage to everyone. A word of caution here: trying too hard to achieve something may, of itself, defeat the effort. Try to give yourself to your mate with as much abandon as possible. Seek to enjoy each other in this God-ordained relationship, and see what happens naturally.

The roles which a man and woman accept and perform in their marriage have a definite effect upon their whole family. Today there is much confusion regarding roles. Lacking a definitive concept of one's own role does not engender a creative, sparkling marriage. To exercise our capacities properly, there must not be a feeling of superiority or inferiority. Husband and wife are to stand side-by-side in an equal and complementary partnership. Each needs a sense of his or her own dignity and worth to fulfill his or her responsibilities adequately. A struggle for victory over the other person, with resulting competition between the two, will be a detriment to achieving unity. The husband's delight needs to be in the unfolding fulfillment of his wife. The wife's primary career should be aiding her husband to be a true man.

Distortion of these roles can be fatal. The most common error of today is the man's abdication of his manhood. The American male seems to have substituted an effort to be a good economic provider for his rightful role as spiritual head, or leader. In this, he has cheated himself and robbed his wife and family. He may fail to achieve command of himself and, from a posture of immaturity, become domineering. The result will be either a dollhouse or a madhouse—not a family. His wife and children are either subdued or rebellious, and cannot be creatively responsive.

The woman's role as the follower is often distorted. She may try to be domineering, which is contrary to her nature. An overbearing wife forfeits true love from her husband. Or she may be a clinging vine, afraid to express her own uniqueness, and thus she robs herself of her true womanhood and she robs her husband of the richness of a genuine marriage. When the roles become distorted, sexuality is replaced by lust, the physical aspect, which too often becomes man's right and woman's duty. Quality in the relationship is lost.

The husband really determines whether the marriage will possess a true sparkle or be a humdrum affair. Yet it is usually more difficult for him to learn his role as lover than it is for the wife to learn her role as responder. The man is the vulnerable one in this partnership, because he is dependent upon his wife's responses for his own fulfillment.

The model for the husband's role is Christ's relationship to the Church, which is called His "bride": "For the husband is the head of the wife, even as Christ is the head of the church . . . Husbands, love your wives, even as Christ also loved the church, and gave himself for it."[6] There are some discernible aspects of Christ's relationship to His people which furnish us clues for the husband-wife relationship. Christ shares His life, His position, His possessions—all that He is and has—with His people, the Church. There is no withholding on His part. He freely gives all! The husband is to share his name, his possessions, and the product of his endeavor—all that he is and has—with his wife. He is to be the protector, the strong umbrella under which his wife and family can grow and unfold their own personalities.

Christ surrenders His welfare, His fulfillment, and His happiness into the hands of the Church. The husband should do the same for his wife. Never can he act solely for himself, because his leadership is necessary to the welfare of all. The husband is very vulnerable here—the price of his leadership is his own vulnerability. The wife is in a position literally to blast his happiness, destroy his dignity and rob him of his manhood.

Christ is the Lover who seeks to meet the needs of His people, and to awaken love and responsiveness in them. The husband should be the lover who meets the needs of his wife. His wife needs security; not simply financial security, but the security of knowing that she is loved deeply and unconditionally. When she knows that her husband really cares about her happiness, she can forget her own pleasures to make him content. The wife must know that her husband needs her, and that she means something special to him. This will leave her free to be herself, because she knows she is accepted.

The wife also needs the strength that her husband can give, both his physical strength and his inner strength. She must know that she can depend on him when she has exhausted her own resources. She must be able to turn to her husband when she is in difficulty. If her husband is fulfilling his role, she will find in him the kind of strength that makes it unnecessary for her to struggle quite so often.

The wife desperately needs for her husband to be a good father to their children.

The husband is to be the lover who draws from his wife

responses she cannot make by will alone. He is to awaken her to her own uniqueness and to her femininity. A girl may be plain-looking until she marries a man who can give her real love. Then she may blossom into a beautiful woman. Conversely, a lovely girl who does not find love in her marriage may quickly lose her beauty. Just as Christ sees the hidden potential in His bride, the Church, the husband sees the hidden beauty in his wife, and seeks to call it forth. He does this in part by continually assuring her that he sees in her something that is very lovely. We have often heard that love is blind, but in reality real love enables the lover to see in the beloved what others do not see.

No man can play his role perfectly, but, if he seriously attempts to perform his role adequately, he is worthy of respect and honor. To do this, he needs the resources that only a vital relationship with Jesus Christ can supply for such a demanding and rewarding role.

The role of the wife is basically that of a *responder* who finds her own fulfillment by fulfilling her husband. She holds the welfare of her entire family in her hands. Her arena is the most important place of all—the home. And a woman who can create an atmosphere of peace and serenity in her home is an artist without competition. She has an almost inexhaustible power to give, which is released when she knows that she is loved.

The wife who responds enthusiastically helps her husband to be a man, and also gives him a sense of his own fidelity. Their relationship will be so meaningful that her husband will know he cannot find what they have together anywhere else. When he sees other women, he will think of his wife and the beauty of their relationship. If she refuses to respond, he will begin to doubt his masculinity and adequacy—like an orchestra leader who motions for the music to begin, and no sounds come forth.

The wife actually helps her huband be the leader by her responsiveness to him. To withhold is to deaden the relationship; to respond enthusiastically is to enliven it. The husband may, in the beginning, be a poor lover and leader.

But, if the wife will "submit (herself) unto (her) own husband, as unto the Lord,"[7] it will have a pronounced effect upon him. I know the meaning of the word "submit" has been ruined by its popular connotation. It does not mean to be a doormat or to deny one's own thoughts, or feelings, or life. The wife must share these thoughts and feelings, and express her own uniqueness. But when speaking to women's groups, I have substituted the word "respond" for "submit" which, I feel, is closer in popular thought to what Paul had in mind in Ephesians. If a man is worth his salt, when he realizes what his wife is giving him, he will seek to be a lover who can meet his wife's needs. But the giving must be without strings attached. If it becomes a swap-out, and not the expression of love freely given and freely received, then it loses its potency for deepening the relationship. One lady asked me, "Which partner must first begin trying to play his or her role adequately for this to work?" My reply was, "The one who recognizes the need first." Everyone has to begin where they are. There is so much hope for even the most troubled marriages, that it is a shame that so many of them end in divorce.

Another important aspect of the wife's role is that she, more than anyone else, reinforces her husband's dreams for success and for his career. Without the wife to build him up after the world has shaken his confidence in himself and shattered his dreams, he would either give up or dream less. She restores his faith in himself. When a man has the security of a wife who is really for him, there is not much that he could not accomplish. She gives him that something he cannot get any place else—completeness.

To play her role, the wife needs to accept her own femininity. She should be glad that she is a woman. The wife must be able to give in to passionate feelings without feeling guilty, and she should make sex attractive to her husband. She must give freely and receive freely.

A wife needs a sense of significance and a sense of her own worth as a person. She often needs to respond even in the midst of confusion. She must be herself, expressing her emotions and communicating her feelings. Her husband desperately depends upon her, whether he acknowledges it or not. He needs her to love him with everything that is in her. The wife has this same dependence on the husband. If she determines to meet his needs, and asks for God's help, she will find her own needs being met as well. If she tries to make him supremely happy, she will find great happiness. She accomplishes this by giving herself.

The place to begin in making marriage sparkle is to ask the Living God to enable you to achieve the kind of marriage that would beget love and creativity. Perhaps a part of this well-known prayer would adequately express the needed response for both husband and wife:

> Divine Master,
> Grant that I may not so much seek to be
> Consoled as to console;
> To be understood as to understand;
> To be loved as to love;
> For it is in giving that we receive;
> It is in pardoning that we are pardoned;
> And it is in dying that we are born to
> eternal life.
>
> St. Francis of Assisi

QUESTIONS

1. What is the purpose of marriage?
2. What makes a good marriage?
3. Where did you meet your husband or wife? What was your first impression of him or her?
4. What does your husband, or wife, need most from you in your present relationship?
5. If you have children, what do you think each one needs from you at present?
6. What is the purpose of sex?

7. Describe the husband/wife roles as you understand them to be.
8. What does the writer mean when he says the wife gives her husband a sense of fidelity and the husband his wife a sense of security?
9. If you are married, what is the greatest thing your marriage has going for it at present?
10. How did you feel when you saw your first-born?
11. Have you ever given God thanks for the gift of your sexuality?
12. What is the difference in love and lust?
13. Why must sex be reserved for a secure relationship such as marriage?
14. How can a couple make the most of the time they have together?
15. What kind of marriage did your parents or parent substitutes have?
16. Do you know a couple who have a really good marriage? What do you see in their relationship that is attractive to you?
17. How do you find the right person for marriage?
18. What do you need to do to make your marriage sparkle?

CHAPTER 9

WHAT ABOUT MY VOCATION?

God made man ruler over all things.

Christianity is a marketplace religion. It is not a mystical idealism unrelated to the issues we face daily. The God revealed ultimately in Jesus of Nazareth is concerned with the everyday tedium of man's existence—including the nitty gritty of daily work. God's redemptive activity in us enters every facet of our experience. Even as He saves us from self-absorption, He keeps our work from becoming meaningless drudgery. Just as we have to turn ourselves over to Christ in faith to find life, so must we turn our work over to Christ to find fulfillment in it. Theoretically, when we commit ourselves to Christ, we commit all. But, practically speaking, most people find they have to give Him one area of their lives at a time.

In conversion, one has the awareness of a relationship in which he experiences forgiveness, acceptance and love. But beyond that initial encounter, the implications of that new relationship must be lived out daily. Christ said, "If anyone chooses to be my disciple, he must say 'No' to self, put the cross on his shoulders daily, and continue to follow me."[1] The words "daily" and "continue" point up our real battle. In the midst of great inspiration, we may resolve to give Christ all, but the real difficulty comes in the aftermath, the daily decision. Our hope is that the same God who touched us in that inspired moment will continue to be with us in our daily life. The promise of Christ is, "I will not leave you."[2] We are assured, therefore, that our resources are sufficient for the tasks at hand!

In examining the Christian implications for work, we need to begin with the affirmation that work is a gift of God. The biblical message begins with God's creative activity. Six days He labors and the seventh He rests from His labor.[3] Man is made in God's image and is commanded to "Be fruitful and increase in number; fill the earth and subdue it. Rule over the fish of the sea and the birds of the air and over every living creature that moves on the ground . . . The Lord God took the man and put him in the Garden of Eden to work it and take care of it."[4] Man is given a place and a task. His place needs his work. He is to participate with God in His creative activity. Man's labor is an expression of his affinity to God. With the fall of man comes the distortion of work. The drudgery, bitterness, and exploitation of man's workaday life is the consequence of his rebellion against God.

The biblical message does not conclude with man's sin, which affects all of creation, but continues with a new work that God is doing. His new work is one of redemption, which also includes all of creation. After the Lord had restored the prostitute at Jacob's well, He said to His disciples, "My food is to do the will of him who sent me and to finish his work."[5] Again Paul declares, "For if anybody is in union with Christ, he is the work of a new creation, the old condition has passed away, a new condition has come."[6] God-in-Christ, through the Holy Spirit, is active in the world today effecting a new creation. The people caught up with Him are to become participants in accomplishing His work of reconciliation.

The marketplace is one of the major frontiers, according to Paul in Ephesians, where a Christian is to exercise this ministry of reconciliation. This ministry is not something tacked onto our occupation. It is more than a simple verbalizing of one's faith, although that is an authentic part. It is a new quality that is interwoven into one's work. The person who has discovered this new life in Christ begins to experience the kind of security that allows him to look at his work realistically and creatively. No longer does his life depend upon any particular job. He is free to be the master of his work, and not a slave to it. Christ has opened to us a new perspective in all of life that can transform any mundane routine into an exciting opportunity for God to make Himself known. No longer is the paycheck the sole motivation for work. This person sees his work as a part of God's creative and redemptive purpose. He knows that God is concerned that people have the necessities for physical well-being. Any constructive contribution to mankind can be a part of God's caring ministry to His world, when the person allows it to be so. If profit is the only motivation for working, a person may make a constructive contribution, but it will fail to have the wholesome effect on him that God intended. Profit is legitimate and necessary, but not at the cost of exploiting people.

This new perspective in Christ opens the way for us to see our work as service to God. Even though we may be committed to a bad situation, this will enable us to find meaning in it. Paul sent the runaway slave, Onesimus, back to Philemon to change the injustice of slavery from within. Both as a slave and as a Christian brother, he returned to Philemon. As a slave to Jesus Christ, he had more freedom in his human slavery than many men have in their human freedom. Paul says:

> You slaves must practice obedience to your earthly masters, with reverence and awe, with sincerity of heart, as you would obey Christ, not serving them as though they were watching you, but as true slaves of Christ, trying to carry out the will of God. Heartily and cheerfully keep on working as slaves, as though it were for the Lord and not for men, for you know that everyone, slave or free, will

get his reward from the Lord for anything good he has done. You slaveowners, too, must maintain the same attitude toward your slaves, and stop threatening them, for you know that their real Lord and yours is in heaven, and that He never shows partiality.[7]

This reality taken seriously would destroy slavery without bloodshed.

Christianity is not the champion of the status quo. Christianity has such revolutionary qualities inherent in it that it will change any society in which Christ is taken seriously. This revolutionary power is, in essence, suffering love.

One who, like Onesimus, sees himself caught up in God's purpose for life and history can afford the risk of change. Christianity has never been dependent upon any economic or political structure. It has survived under all kinds of governments—and will continue to do so. But with the freedom enjoyed today in America, a person has plenty of choice in his work. A friend, who has been successful over the years, came to me about a decision concerning two business ventures. One offered him a partnership in a new company which could mean big money in a short time. The other offered him the opportunity to be what he really wanted to be, a stockbroker, but without the promise of quick financial gain. He was in his middle thirties. I suggested that financial gain was not reason enough for a man to sell himself short of his dreams. If he really wanted to be a stockbroker, I thought he should give it a try. We covenanted together to pray about his decision. He finally chose to be a stockbroker, a goal which has given him real satisfaction. He told me later that the other company had not panned out to be as successful as anticipated. No one should sell himself short, for any reason!

Work, as the gift of God, furnishes us an arena in which we can express ourselves and experience a sense of accomplishment. This feeling is essential to one's personal well-being. In reality, our work becomes an extension of our own personality. This is true for the laborer, the businessman, the professional person, and the housewife. For example, we learned in Japan that the flower arrangement expresses the attitude present in that home on that particular day. If there has been an argument or a celebration—whatever the mood—it is expressed by flowers. The American home may not be so expressively decorated with flower arrangements, but there are a million other ways the climate within is reflected. The home becomes an expression of the woman's feelings and personality, and is the arena for her loving, creative contribution to her family. This can give meaning even to scraping dried egg yolk from a saucer. Anything that can do that is worth pursuing.

To see one's work as an extension of his or her own personality is to realize its significance and importance. This is not the arena for "goofing off," because we are affected by our attitude and response to it, and so are others around us. Work is one of the main stages where the real drama of human life is going on.

Reuel Howe points out in his book, *The Creative Years*, that "The quality of the work and its significance as a free contribution to life is not dependent upon the nature of the work but upon the character of the workman."[8] This was vividly demonstrated to me by a junior high school janitor named Emmett. Emmett could call every kid in that school by his first name. He always went the second mile in every job he was asked to do, either by the administration or by the teachers. Everyone loved and respected Emmett. As a student I stayed after school occasionally to help him dust erasers, just to be with him. He has been my friend for eighteen years, and I have never seen any man express more dignity and purpose in his work than Emmett. It is the man who makes the job, and not the job the man!

Seeing our work as service to God and mankind brings a whole-heartedness to the occupation. When I was in college I worked part-time during school and full-time in the summer at a service station. For months I lived for the weekends when I could speak a word for God in a church. I knew God was interested in my preaching, but how could He care about my car washing? I could not get God into that service station. How could the God who created the universe and who sustains it be interested in a service station? The glory of it all is that He is interested in us and in our work, whatever it may be!

I had worked at the station about three years when the owner became a Christian. After that, I think we had more church Monday through Saturday at that station than some churches have on Sunday. We dialogued about our feelings, experiences and ideas. We discussed the Scriptures. But, most of all, we had a ball making that station an expression of our ministry. When a car left the highway to come into our drive, we hit the door at a trot. By the time that car stopped, one of us was standing at the driver's window saying, "Yes, sir!" We could fill that car with gas, check under the hood, clean the windshield and have the ticket made out before the driver could get cold drinks for his family! The two of us went out of our way to serve the customers, and had a great time doing it. Our attitude and eagerness to be of service had an amazing effect on them. Enthusiasm is contagious! Before long, Lloyd had almost more business than he could handle. The more you give the more you receive. That is the law of life! I still loved my weekend ministry (pastoring a small country church), but I also enjoyed translating the messages I preached into concrete experience in that station during the week.

To avoid confusion, I would like to define two words for the purpose of this book. In modern usage these are usually considered synonymous. One word is "vocation," which I am using as God's call to every man to become His person. The other word is "occupation" ("work," "job," "career")—that activity in which he is engaged.

People have different gifts, and blessed is the person who recognizes his talents and uses them. We may feel called by God to our occupation or we may not. God's providence and our choice are determinative factors in choosing a career. But

God *calls* everyone to be His person. This is our common vocation. Our occupation, then, becomes the arena in which our vocation is expressed.

According to Acts, chapter eleven, the believers were first called Christians in Antioch. Paul and Barnabas had labored for a whole year, teaching and equipping the laity of the church. The impact that these believers had upon their peers and their society resulted in their being called Christians. They were known as "followers of Christ." Christian is a vocational word. Their calling was to be God's person, though they earned their livelihood in many different ways. Certainly, the kind of persons that they were carried over into the work they did, and it made their work a service to God and mankind. David Maitland points out that "This means that there is no God-preferred work. The clergy have not entered upon labors which assume their superiority to the laity. Nor, on the other hand, is the clergyman any more accountable to serve God responsibly in his work than is any Christian in his. Work is of the order of God."[9] The distinction between clergy and laity is functional only. The clergy are called from among the laity (the people of God) to give up their legitimate pursuits of a particular work to be made an equipper, or coach, to help the laity exercise their ministry in and to the world.

Paul entreats us to "walk worthy of the vocation wherewith ye are called."[10] Our calling is to be Christian, and to "walk worthy" is to allow the whole of life to be brought into harmony with our position as sons of God.

In relation to work there needs to be a word concerning rest and relaxation. The fourth commandment is, "Six days shalt thou labor, and do thy work: But the seventh day is the Sabbath of the Lord thy God: in it thou shalt not do any work."[11] David Redding points out:

> Overwork is another sin that makes us suffer biologically. We are all more tolerant of the man who is killing himself with work than the one who is killing himself by running away from it, but both

extremes are immoral, and run up the rates of hospitalization insurance. A man can work his way to the hospital as well as to hell. The speaker may feel complimented when he is introduced as one who "works like a horse," but is that healthy for a man? Hyperactivity can be pathological. "He's a very busy man" may be an insult, depending on what a man is busy about—whether he works to avoid the emptiness in his soul, or to keep from having to sit down and think his life through on a Sunday afternoon.

What is one's work doing to the rest of the family? Overwork is often the work of pride. One mother slaves away to make herself indispensable, another to indulge a martyr complex . . . Overwork kills more Americans than cars do. We have become perpetual-motion machines in our frantic flight from God. A job was made for a man and not a man for a job.[12]

God made the Sabbath for people. The purpose of the Sabbath is to give us rest from our labors—to break the routine, to change the pace—so we can be reminded all over again that we are spiritual beings with great destinies. To take away our rest, our reflectiveness and our awareness of being spiritual beings would be to reduce us to the "work horse" level, and, thus, stifle our creativity and kill our spirit. Charles Allen, in his book, *God's Psychiatry*, says with regard to the Sabbath:

> God gave us the day, not as a time of prohibitions but rather to give us opportunity for the finest and most important things of life. An old miner once explained to a visitor, "I let my mules spend one day a week outside the mines to keep them from going blind." And the person who does not spend time away from the daily grind of life goes blind in his soul. The philosopher Santayana tells us, "A fanatic

is one who, having lost sight of his aim, redoubles his effort." And much of the feverish haste we see today is by aimless, purposeless people. God says we need a day a week to keep our aim. Or, as Carylye put it, "The man who does not habitually worship is but a pair of spectacles behind which there is no eye."[13]

In America we are such activists that we feel if we are not doing something we are wasting time. We need to learn how to be still and allow the creative resources of our personality to be replenished. The Lord calls us to "Be still, and know that I am God."[14] This kind of inner stillness is essential for the growth and development of a healthy personality. Someone has pointed out that noisy waters are shallow, but that still waters run deep.

Many people find silence almost unbearable. A few years ago, in a retreat at Dayspring, the retreat center for the Church of the Savior in Washington, D.C., we observed three days of silence. One minister was so bugged by it, that he went to his car, took out his maps and planned his next summer's vacation. Brief periods of silence have been one of the most productive experiences of my own retreat ministry. One can be so involved in doing good work that he may forget the very things which would enable him to do the best work.

I have already mentioned one of the most foolish things that I have ever done — not taking a vacation for five years. It affected the quality of my ministry, stifling my creativity and awareness. Take some time away from it all. It will benefit everyone concerned. God purposes that we enjoy life, both the work and the play. Creation bears witness to this. So much beauty is displayed everywhere for the person who has eyes to see.

By a person's work, he acquires money and property. How should a person relate to his possessions? The way we answer this question will be one of the most determinative factors in our life. History bears witness to the significant role that possessions play in human life. There has always been tension between the "haves" and "have-nots," and from this tension have come revolutions and war.

To begin with, it should be noted that money is not evil. It is the love of money that is evil. We were made to love people and to use things. When that order is reversed, we are in trouble. We need to be reminded that a poor man can love money as much as a rich man. Having money is no prerequisite for loving money. It is true that the person with great wealth has some problems unique to him. It takes a spiritually mature person to handle great wealth, and to keep his wealth from handling him.

Wealth is a relative thing, too. I have never considered myself a rich man—monetarily. But, in India, Hong Kong, and Thailand I suddenly realized that, in relation to the majority of those people, I was a wealthy man. Some of the sights I witnessed there are reproduced in our own country as well, but in more isolated instances. Nevertheless, this experience gave me a new perspective of plenty and its accompanying stewardship.

When a man in the crowd asked Jesus to make his brother share his inheritance with him, Jesus answered, "Be ever on the alert and always on your guard against every form of greed, because a man's life does not consist of his possessions, even though they are abundant."[15] A man's life does not consist of his possessions, but in his relationship to Jesus Christ. To make the acquiring of things an end in itself is to miss real life. Eavey, in *Practical Christian Ethics*, points out:

> Actually, property and wealth are of only secondary and passing importance, not part of the true and abiding self. "The last robe that is made for one has no pockets," says an Italian proverb. Ambition to get rich and the consequent pursuit of wealth ministers to the baser passions of our nature. It engenders selfishness; it feeds pride; it inspires a false sense of security; it does damage to all the

nobler feelings and the higher aspirations of the heart. "When money is not a servant, it is a master," says another Italian proverb, and it is a hard master.[16]

Our ownership of property is not absolute. The Psalmist declares, "The earth is the Lord's and everything in it, the world, and all who live in it."[17] We have the right to *use* property as an expression of ourselves and to meet human need, but we do not *own* anything. The commandment, "Thou shalt not steal,"[18] is a safeguard for use of property that comes into our possession. It is the way we use our possessions that is most significant, and not the quantity of our possessions. Nat Tracy, Professor of Philosophy and Bible at Howard Payne University for twenty-five years, would say, "If you want to lay up treasure in heaven, invest in people." I am inclined to agree with him. The way we use our property affects our character eternally.

The spiritual exercise of tithing set out in the Old Testament is purposed to teach our stubborn hearts that we do not own anything, but that we are owned of God. If this lesson were put into practice, it would eliminate many ulcers and heart attacks. We would see that we are not fighting this battle alone. We could relax and trust God for help and direction.

Once the basic lesson of tithing is learned, a person is ready for Divine partnership as presented in the New Testament. He knows that he belongs to God, and all he has belongs to God. He offers himself, his family, his work and his possessions to God that God might make Himself known to His world through these avenues. This does not impoverish the person who offers himself in this fashion. Quite the contrary. He is enriched and fulfilled beyond anything he himself could do, and his whole life becomes a part of God's eternal purpose.

QUESTIONS

1. Do you see work as a gift of God or as a necessary evil?
2. How can Christ free a person to be creative and productive in his work?
3. Do you see your work as an extension of your own personality? What implications come to you if this is true?
4. What is the primary motivation in your work?
5. Is money evil? Or the love of money?
6. Which is most important, being or doing? Are both important in maturity?
7. Do you enjoy your work?
8. Are you a "workaholic"—working all the time?
9. Can you play without feeling guilty?
10. What is the essence of the revolutionary power in Christianity?
11. Does the job make the person or the person the job?
12. Are all of God's people *called* to be His in the world or is this true of just the clergy?
13. Is there a God-preferred work?
14. What is the purpose of the Sabbath?
15. Does your family enjoy vacationing together?
16. What is the purpose for the spiritual exercise of tithing?
17. What does it mean to enter into partnership with God in all things?

CHAPTER 10

NOT FOR MY SAKE ALONE

He that is greatest among you shall be your servant.

When God gets hold of someone, it is not for his sake alone. It is through this one life that He purposes to touch others in a redemptive way. God is sharing His life with us, and the quality of His life is self-giving. Thus, when one is touched and transformed by God, he shares in His self-giving nature as well. In the Scriptures every person who is called and who responds to that call is impelled to pour himself out for others.

When God called Abraham, it was to leave the security of his home and to become a sojourner in a strange country so that through his seed God could bless all the nations of the earth. When God called to Moses out of the burning bush, it was not to stay on the mountain and enjoy God; it was to go back to Egypt, at the risk of his own life, to be God's man—to lead the children of Israel out of slavery and into the promised land. This was a long and difficult task, but in it he found himself and gave his people a new start.

And God called Israel as a nation, not to favoritism, but to servanthood. He put her in the midst of the Fertile Crescent, so that every nation would be aware of her. In conflict and in commerce the nations traveled through her land. God purposed to demonstrate in Israel what He wanted to do in all nations. But, Israel, though truly God's "chosen people," refused to respond to His call to servanthood, and believed herself to be, instead, God's "favorite people"—entitled to special privileges without obligation.

In the New Testament, Christ said to the men He had called, "You have not chosen me; I have chosen you, and appointed you to go and bear fruit, that your fruit may remain too, so that the Father may grant you, as bearers of my name, whatever you ask Him for."[1] These men were chosen to participate in God's redemptive enterprise, not to escape involvement, or be His "favorites."

On the Damascus road, when Saul of Tarsus was struck blind by the resurrected Christ, he was instructed to go on to Damascus and there he would be told what to do. God spoke to Ananias in a vision and told him to seek out Saul of Taursus. Ananias was reluctant, because of the evil reports he had received concerning this man. The Lord said to Ananias, "Go! This man is my chosen instrument to carry my name before the Gentiles and their kings and before the people of Israel: I will show him how much he must suffer for my name."[2] Saul, who became known as Paul, a servant of Jesus Christ, was called to bear the name of Christ to the Gentiles, to men in high places and to Israel herself. This call would involve great suffering—and it did. One might ask, "Was it worth it?" Paul answers for himself. In his letter to the church at Philippi, he gives his witness. In it he expresses the deepest feelings of his heart.

> For we are the true circumcision, who by the Spirit of God worship Him, who take pride in Jesus Christ only, and do not rely on outward privileges, though I too might rely on these. If anyone thinks that he can rely on outward privileges, far more might I do so: circumcised when I was a week old; a descendant of Israel; a member of the tribe of Benjamin; a Hebrew, a son of Hebrews. Measured by the standard set by the law, I was a Pharisee; by the standard set by zeal, I was a persecutor of the church, and measured by the uprightness reached by keeping the law, I was faultless. But for Christ's sake I have counted all that was gain to me as loss. Yes, indeed, I certainly do count everything as loss

compared with the priceless privilege of knowing Christ Jesus my Lord. For His sake I have lost everything, and value it all as mere refuse, in order to gain Christ and be actually in union with Him, not having a supposed right standing with God which depends on my doing what the law commands, but one that comes through faith in Christ, the real right standing with God which originates from Him and rests on faith. Yes, I long to come to know Him; that is, the power of His resurrection and so to share with Him His sufferings as to be continuously transformed by His death, in the hope of attaining, in some measure, the resurrection that lifts me out from among the dead. It is not a fact that I have already secured it or already reached perfection, but I am pressing on to see if I can capture it, the ideal for which I was captured by Christ Jesus. Brothers, I do not think that I have captured it yet, but here is my one aspiration, so forgetting what is behind me and reaching out for what is ahead of me, I am pressing onward toward the goal, to win the prize to which God through Jesus Christ is calling us upward.[3]

This does not sound like a disappointed or dejected man. Rather, it is the testimony of a man who is almost beside himself with the excitement of being involved with Jesus Christ.

It is a wonderful, and sometimes woeful, thing to be caught up in the hands of the Living God. It is wonderful, because we were made for Him. He does not seek to exploit us, but to make us sons who share in His character and life. It is woeful, because He will not leave us to our own triviality and self-centeredness. He is going to do something great in us, even if He has to break every bone in our body to do it. His love is not indulgent. It has strength and discipline in it.

One reason that we might experience joylessness in our

commitment to Christ is that we lose sight of servanthood. We may become so wrapped up in our own well-being, having our own needs met, pursuing our own maturity that we lose sight of those around us who also have needs. A fact of life is that we get what we give. If we selfishly pursue our own ends, we will live lonely, unfulfilled lives. But, if we reach out to others, seeking to meet their needs, we will find our needs being met—and then some. Our openness and growth are important, because we can only give that which we possess. But we must be generous with what we have within us if we are going to continue to experience growth.

My friend was forced to move to another state by the company he worked for. For a time after his move, he was very discouraged about his new location, his work and his walk with Christ. Later he learned that several families in his new neighborhood were in trouble, and some of them shared their difficulties with him. He and his wife became involved in trying to help these people that life had put next to them. As a result, a sharing group was formed. He wrote me a twelve-page letter, trying to communicate to me the joy he was experiencing by seeking to be Christ's man in that neighborhood. He wrote, "I guess if some time we could be obedient to God and let Him have more of our lives, and quit trying to run our own lives so much of the time, we probably would be surprised what He would do. In spite of everything He has placed us in the most unique situation we've ever been . . . I think this is going to be one of the greatest challenges that we've ever had—trying to be caught up with God in ministering to these people."

It is amazing the excitement that servanthood brings!

From God's perspective, the criterion for greatness is servanthood. The world's idea of greatness is the person who has the most people looking up to him and serving him, but the biblical picture of greatness is the person who can and does serve the most. Christ said, "The greatest among you will be your servant."[4]

Who is the greatest servant in the world? Beyond question, God is!

The biblical picture of God is not one of Him being withdrawn from His world and blithely going about His other affairs. John declares of Christ, who was God in human flesh, "Through him all things were made; without him nothing was made that has been made . . . He was in the world, and though the world was made through him, the world did not recognize him."[5] Paul declares of this same God-man, "For by him all things were created: things in heaven and on earth, visible and invisible, whether thrones or powers or rulers or authorities; all things were created by him and for him. He is before all things, and in him all things hold together."[6] It is by Him that all things are held together. If He were to release it for a moment this universe would disintegrate. He has not abandoned His world. It is still His. He is in it—serving, loving, touching, and caring for those who love Him as well as those who hate Him. With Him there is no partiality and no withholding. He serves all. He gives Himself freely to all. That is Love's Way! He even provides us with the means to resist, if we so choose. It is through Him that all people have the ingredients necessary for life, whether they choose to live for Him or against Him.

The devil is the usurper in this world. He acts as though it were his world, and sometimes it looks as though it is. But he has been decisively defeated in the Christ-event, although he has not yet been expelled from the world.[7]

In washing the disciples' feet, Christ gives an example of the greatness of servanthood, which is the core of His whole ministry:

> So when he had washed their feet and had put on His clothes and taken His place at the table, He said to them again: "Do you understand what I have done to you? You call me Teacher and Lord, and you are right in calling me so, for that is what I am. If I then, your Lord and Teacher, have washed your feet, you too ought to wash one another's feet. For

> I have set you an example, in order that you may practice what I have done to you. I most solemnly say to you, no slave is superior to his master, and no messenger is greater than the man who sends him . . ."[8]

He does not call us to do what He Himself has not done. Rather, He calls us to participate with Him. He cares that even the unbeliever has a better life. He is not saving us out of the world and leaving the rest of the world to its own destruction. He is saving us out of the world to send us back into the world to be the light that can penetrate, heal, reveal, and to be the salt that can add flavor to all of life.

If we had been in that upper room, secretly wanting to be top man, and had the God-man stooped to wash our feet, it would have melted some of the iceberg within—if there was any hope for us at all. That is exactly what He is doing for every one of us right now. He serves us, so we can see, feel, think, dream, love, live! He is laboring behind the scenes to give us a chance at life and to bring us to the place where we can be caught up in His great purpose. It is this kind of servant-love that becomes suffering-love to woo us from our self-centeredness into the life of God. When that same kind of servant-love is embodied in us, the "good news" of Jesus Christ is vividly demonstrated to the world. When we stoop to serve for the same reason that God stoops to serve, we will be confronted again by the Living Christ. For the word will again become flesh in us, and the Spirit of God will use us to impart to men the reality of a loving God.

He calls us to minister, and He furnishes the essential resources and dynamics to make us effective. Paul declares, "For it is God Himself who is at work in you to help you desire it as well as do it."[9]

I spent three days with Dr. Bob Pierce, the founder of World Vision, about ten years ago. I had never seen a man with such compassion for needy and suffering humanity. An associate of his told me that Dr. Bob had been in poor health, and at that time had prayed, asking God to send him to the neediest place in the world for the last days of his ministry. As a result of such concern, he had been in Vietnam for three years, working with orphans, refugees, and the wounded.

Dr. Pierce told me that when he was in college, he saw a ministerial student turn down an invitation to preach in a church, because that church was not large enough for him. He said, "I went to my room and got down on my knees and prayed, 'Lord, when better men than I who ought to do the job, won't, then let me do it.' " If more of us had that spirit, our world would not be in the turmoil that it is in today. Through Dr. Pierce's ministry, thousands of orphans and distressed people have found help and love—and the Christ from whom it flows.

Dr. Bob remarked to me, "I have nothing, but when God calls me to a task He furnishes the resources for accomplishing that task." I witnessed the truth of his words in the three days that I was with him. He was on his way back to Vietnam and needed to take one hundred wheel chairs with him for the wounded Vietnamese. In one afternoon the Lord provided $7500.00 for the wheel chairs. Also, he was working on a project that would give aid and employment to the Vietnamese and he needed a quarter of a million dollars with which to begin. He told the head of a large company, who was selling him the raw materials, "I have nothing; but my Father is rich." As sure as I live, his Father is rich! The quarter of a million dollars was provided. This man was a fool for Christ and His world, and God gave him the resources for the task.

Dr. Bob told me one very moving story which illustrates the real motivation of this man's heart. He gave some Vietcong prisoners crutches and watched them walk on those crutches back to their own people in a prisoner-of-war exchange. Jesus said, "Verily I say unto you, Inasmuch as ye have done it unto one of the least of these my brethren, ye have done it unto me."[10] Who the person was did not matter to Dr. Bob. It was the need that qualified a person for his help.

Dr. Bob Pierce taught me much about love for people and faith in God. When we parted there were no words for either of us to speak. We wept and embraced and went our separate ways. I will never forget him, and I hope never to forget what he taught me about love and faith by his life.

All of us will not be called to a World Vision ministry, but all of us will be called to a ministry of love and caring. And the best place to begin is where we are, with the people in our own sphere of influence. One of the men in my pastorate became excited about Christ and wanted to get involved in ministry. He came to see me one day, troubled about where he lived. He said, "I may need to move to town. I just don't have anyone out there to minister to." (He lived about six miles out in the country.) We prayed together about this matter and asked the Lord to make clear his place of ministry.

Less than two weeks later this same man came to our house all excited. A neighbor had come to buy a calf, and while he was there they began to talk about some personal problems. This opened the door for these two men to really get acquainted, although they had known each other for years. Feed salesmen came by, and others to do work on the farm. All of a sudden this fellow began to be aware of people who had been right there in his world all along. And these people had needs.

This is true of all of us! We look for a glamorous place to perform some dramatic ministry, when there is real need all around us. In fact, the best place to begin is with one's own family. Sometimes one steps over his own wife and children to get out there "somewhere" to tell the world that God loves them. One night, while I was lying in the middle of the floor wrestling with our two boys (David, aged seven, and Stephen, two-and-one-half), our little girl, almost four, came up and hit me with a toy. I was a little upset by this, both because it hurt and because we were teaching the children not to hit. I went with her into the bedroom and asked her why she had hit me. Her answer went straight to my heart: "I want to play with daddy, too." She needed some of my attention that the boys were getting. A little later we announced to the boys that Shawna Lee and daddy were going to have a time together. We lay across the bed and talked. She told me one of the stories we had previously read to her. She told me about her new dress and asked when we were going to Pa Pa's house. It was a delightful conversation and it changed her entire attitude. I had the feeling that this conversation was the most significant part of my entire day, although I had addressed a group and had counseled with three people. May God help us to start at home with our caring ministry.

We are dependent upon God to make us into the kind of servants He needs for His world. We will fail miserably if we try to *act* like His servant. The Christian is made by God and is not the product of self-effort. The Scriptures declare, "We are God's workmanship, created in Christ Jesus to do good works, which God prepared in advance for us to do."[11] It is only Christ in us, working through us, that will make us effective servants.

One mark of the servant of Jesus Christ is that he possesses the spirit of a son. We are to be servants, but with a filial spirit. This may seem like hair-splitting, but there is as much difference in the spirit of servitude and the spirit of sonship as between daylight and darkness. In the parable of the prodigal son the elder brother had a spirit of servitude, which caused him to begrudge his brother for receiving unmerited love. This elder brother had remained at home, not because he authentically shared his father's interests, but to receive a greater inheritance. The spirit of servitude labors for reward, as does a hireling. The motivation is external pressure, "fear of punishment" or "hope of reward." There can be no enthusiasm or joy, and the work will be dull and boring. The spirit of servitude can risk little. Great caution must be exercised for fear of making a mistake and suffering severe consequences. In short, to be under the spirit of servitude is to be enslaved.

To have the son-spirit is to be liberated for one's own expression of life. The motivation is from within. There is an identity between the son and the father, and the son realizes that what is the father's, belongs to him—not by right of merit, but because of love. The son acts for the same reason that the father acts, because it is his character to do so. No one need pay him. He does not feel that he has to do it. He wants to do it.

We have exercised the son-spirit when we have ministered to someone, not because we felt we had to, but for the sheer delight of serving. Suppose we had a servant and a son in our house, and our son truly had a filial spirit. Though the two shared the work equally, there would be a world of difference in their attitudes. We are the sons of God, called to participate in His ministry to the world! Jesus said to His disciples, "I no longer call you slaves, because the slave does not know what his master is doing; I now call you friends, because I have told you everything that I have learned from my Father."[12] For God to call us "friends" is grace beyond compare!

One night while driving home from Bible study I unconsciously stumbled into the meaning of the son-spirit. Those who know me know that I am not the world's best singer. But when I am alone, I do sing—believe it or not. This particular night the response of the group in the Bible study had been great, and there was such evidence of Christ healing and opening eyes that had been shut tight, that I could hardly believe it. I was driving back to Dallas and singing up a storm. Without thought, I uttered a prayer. My prayer was, "Lord, You don't have to remember that I was in Temple tonight. Just being there and seeing You work was its own reward." Then it hit me. God had really been at work in my life that night as well. I felt deeply as never before that I was His son as the result of His grace, getting a bit of the kick out of it that He must get. I sobbed a prayer of thanksgiving.

When it comes to specific ministries, I can only offer suggestions in a few areas. It is Christ who calls us to minister, and life furnishes plenty of opportunities. We must be alert and creative in our ministry. Sometimes the Lord will give us an impression of what we should do; sometimes He leaves it to our ingenuity and remains more behind the scenes. He comes to us in a fashion and says, "Son, see that world around you? Let's you and I do something redemptive in it." Sometimes He may even ask, "Where do you want to start?" We are not robots that He manipulates. We have been called into loving participation with Him. He has not hired us or threatened in order to make us work. He loves us into ministry!

There are some simple things that we can do daily that may be tremendously helpful to those around us. We can participate in Christ's ministry of listening. God listens to all that men have to say. But many people do not recognize this, because they have never been listened to by another human being. We can ask the Lord to help us hear what people are saying, both by their words and by their actions.

We can ask Christ to enable us to see people as persons and not as things. We can ask Christ to help us reach out to others in love and acceptance.

We can ask Christ for an opportunity to gossip the "good news" that we have found in Him with as much freedom and excitement as grandparents have in gossiping about their grandchildren.

We can ask Christ to enable us to recognize where we may have wronged another and to give us courage to apologize and make restitution.

We can engage in the ministry of prayer. We can pray for certain individuals and for specific needs they have.

Each of us needs to participate in Bible study of some kind. We need our own devotional time with the Scriptures to keep our perspective clear, and we need some kind of dialogue with others as we study the Scriptures and share our personal struggles. This is being done in churches, in homes, in offices all across our country today. To miss out on the way God is moving at the grass roots level today is to miss out on what may be the greatest spiritual awakening since the Reformation.

Christ may call us to a specific task through some need

in the world. He may call us to a job too great for one person to tackle alone. But with that call, He will bring others to participate with us. If we could only believe that He is running the show and trust Him, we could move mountains with Him.

Do not wait for a nudge from heaven to begin ministering. By faith, reach out with love to those near you, and all of heaven will support you.

QUESTIONS

1. What does the writer mean when he says, "When God gets hold of a person, it is not for his sake alone?" Has this been true in your life?
2. Why did God choose Israel? Christ His disciples? And Saul on the road to Damascus?
3. What produces joylessness in our commitment to Christ?
4. What is God's criterion for greatness?
5. Who is the greatest servant in the world today?
6. Have you ever sensed that God was washing your feet that you might have the chance to be more than you have been?
7. What is the shape of your ministry at present?
8. What does it mean to possess a son-spirit?
9. Have you ever done something for another just for the sheer delight of serving that other person?
10. Have you ever consciously participated in Christ's listening ministry?
11. List some simple ways one could minister out of his daily contact with people. Which ones are you willing to engage in?

CHAPTER 11

FINDING AN ADEQUATE MOTIVATION FOR THE JOURNEY

You must love the Lord your God with all your heart, and with all your soul, and with all your mind. This is the greatest and the most important commandment.

I have a friend who owns an insurance agency in Dallas. He said to me, "The biggest problem in selling insurance is motivation. The salesmen usually start out with enthusiasm, because they see a real challenge. But, fifty percent of them fall by the wayside the first year. The continuing motivation is not there." This is the problem that most businesses face. All kinds of motivation gimmicks have been devised by advertising and management personnel to propel people into action. Some of these gimmicks work quite well for a short time; then some new idea must be introduced to sustain the momentum. Occasionally, you run across a person who really loves his work, and finds real satisfaction in it. He may need to regain his perspective from time to time, but he does not need tricks to prod him into production. He does what he does because he loves it, and because he finds meaning and fulfillment in it. This illustrates a basic truth about people. Rational knowledge is necessary if we are to act, but it is not adequate to furnish the dynamics which thrust us into action. We are not primarily rational beings. If we were, knowledge would be sufficient for action. The truth is that all of us have a great deal of information—in almost every area of life—that we are not willing to act upon.

People are by nature value-pursuing creatures. We use our reason to pursue what we esteem. It can be said that the most determinative thing about us is whom and what we love. The attitude of our heart predetermines what we see and experience. This is why one person sees the work of God in nature, and another vehemently declares the absence of God in nature. Both may examine the same phenomena, but one perceives with the eyes of belief, and the other with the eyes of unbelief. There is no middle ground, no pure objectivity for anyone in the realm of personal action. Our values shape the world we see, hear, feel, and contemplate. Therefore, when we lose faith, despair and pessimism produce a "Why try?" attitude. But faith can see distressing circumstances as challenges and awaken us to creative action.

The Christian is called to be God's person in this hostile world and he is commissioned to try to remake this world on the pattern of heaven. This task will never be fully accomplished before the Lord's return. But in accepting this goal and attempting to reach it, we will see that God is concerned with the total of man's life, and that when He touches us we become concerned with the whole of man's existence as well. In the midst of the ever increasing conflict between good and evil, God is working out His purposes. The wheat and the tares are growing side by side, and they shall continue to do so until the Judgment.

To accept and to pursue the task to which God has called us demands a great motivation. Because they lack motivation, many who begin the Christian venture fizzle quickly. The initial excitement that comes to the new convert is usually lost in the long uphill pull. A new Christian may feel that he can change the world, and he sets out to do just that. Before long he finds that the world is a tougher nut to crack than he realized. It is at this point of disillusionment that he needs to turn to God for adequate motivation for the difficult and challenging task ahead.

If the glow of commitment begins to dim, we feel we must keep on keeping on, but it becomes a chore instead of a joy. Our motivation begins to be more negative than positive. After a time, many of us find that our reason for continuing is no more than "fear of punishment" and "hope of reward"—from both God and man. This prods us into action, but it will be without spontaneity or creativity. It will be activity calculated to gain an advantageous position for receiving rewards or escaping punishment.

Some of us may find that our excuse for continuing is social pressure that favors involvement in religious activities. "It's the proper thing to do." We fear rejection by a certain segment of society if we are not involved. Or, perhaps, we seek to enhance our image with this group by increasing our activity. Our need for acceptance may keep us going and it may even generate a measure of enthusiasm. But it will never be enough to sustain us.

For some, the motivation may simply be to keep the peace. If we remain "faithful" to certain activities, everyone is happy and we all drift tranquilly, but aimlessly, downstream, with no friction, and even less joy, in life.

None of these motivations will be sufficient for the challenge of keeping on. Fear of punishment and hope of reward stifle faith and eliminate risk. To be caught up in these motivations is to become paralyzed, unable to take any action without great need for quoting a specific verse of Scripture for each decision to avoid the possibility of making a mistake. In theological circles this is usually called "legalism." I am not minimizing the Scriptures. The more we hide the Word of God in our hearts the better equipped we will be. But the Scriptures are not intended to be legal contracts or detailed blueprints for our every action. The Scripture's purpose is to lead us to a personal relationship with their Author. The promises of God are a genuine source of encouragement, but they do not come apart from a personal relationship with Him. Our greatest security and assurance comes in our continuing relationship with Jesus Christ and in His ability to finish what He has begun in us.

The most creative, dynamic motivation that exists is love. It is love alone that will suffice for the battle we face. It is a love which runs as deep as life itself for Jesus Christ and for what He purposes that will be the only adequate motivation for the Christian. The classic example of this love in the Old Testament is Abraham offering his son, Isaac. Abraham did not start out with this passionate kind of love for God. He began with a simple faith. This simple faith evolved into the exercise of a love affair between Abraham and his God. Finally, the love and trust that he had for the God who called him, ran so deep that he withheld nothing from Him. He offered the son who was dearer to him than life itself. God's response to such trust and love was:

> "I swear by myself," declares the Lord, "that because you have done this, and have not withheld your son, your only son, I will surely bless you and make your descendants as numerous as the stars in the sky, and as the sand of the seashore. Your descendants will take possession of the cities of their enemies, and through your offspring all the nations on earth will be blessed, because you have obeyed me."[11]

God did something great in Abraham, because Abraham was willing for Him to do it.

In the New Testament, the classic example of the need for a great love is found in the twenty-first chapter of John's gospel. Simon Peter had, prior to the crucifixion, made promises which he could not keep. He was in that naive state of believing that his life was adequate. In the upper room, when Christ indicated that He would be betrayed and that they would all forsake Him, Peter boasted that he was ready to go to prison and to death with Him. He assured the Lord that he could be counted on when the going became rough. Jesus responded by saying, "Peter, you do not know yourself yet, do you? Before the rooster crows you will deny Me three times."[2] Peter did deny Him, the third time cursing and swearing that he did not know the man: "The Lord turned and looked straight at Peter. Then Peter remembered the word the Lord had spoken to him: 'Before the rooster crows today, you will disown me three times.' And he went out and wept bitterly."[3] After Peter blew it, he saw the same accepting love in the face of Christ that he had seen from the very beginning—and it broke him up. He went out and wept bitter tears of repentance. Now he knew what unconditional love, acceptance and forgiveness were all about.

It is a strange thing, but most of us seem to have to sin against love before we can really accept love. Only when we *recognize* that we have blown it does the full impact of the unconditional acceptance, unconditional love, and unconditional forgiveness God offers penetrate the deeper levels of our being and melt the coldness of our hearts. To see what Peter saw in the face of Christ will either awaken a deep, passionate love for Him within us, or it will destroy our ability to love at all—as in the case of Judas Iscariot.

When the resurrected Lord confronted Peter a little later, He did not ask Peter to promise never to deny Him again. He was concerned with only one thing: "Simon, son of John, do you truly love me?"[4] If our love for Christ is real, then He can do the rest in and through us.

Peter's response to this question is not as naive as it was before his denial. To understand the reality of this, we need to understand the play on words in the dialogue between Christ and Peter in the twenty-first chapter of John. This is even more apparent in the Greek text. Christ is using *agape*, which we translate "love," and Peter is using *phileo*, which we also translate "love." *Phileo* is a love between friends in which there is a mutual delight in the relationship. *Agape* is totally other-centered, and it is motivated by a sense of the preciousness of the one loved.

Christ is asking, "Do you love Me with the kind of love that I have loved you with?" Peter is responding, "Lord, I love You as a friend, but I am not capable of giving You the kind of love that You have given me." Christ responds, "Feed my little lambs." Then again, "Feed my sheep." He is calling Simon to share with Him in His enterprise, if he has any love at all. If there is no love, there will be no participation. If there is little love, there will be some participation. But if there is great love, then there will be sacrificial participation.

Twice Christ asks Simon about *agape* and twice Simon responds with *phileo*. The third time Jesus uses the word Simon has been using and asks, "Are you sure you are My friend?" When real love is questioned, it makes itself known. Peter responds, "Lord, You know all things; You know that I am Your friend." The Lord then responds, " 'I tell you the truth, when you were younger, you dressed yourself and went where you wanted, but when you are old, you will stretch out your hands, and someone else will dress you and lead you where you do not want to go.' Jesus said this to indicate the kind of death by which Peter would glorify God."[5] The Lord was saying to him that when he was immature, with a shallow kind of naive love, he could call his own shots. But as he matures and becomes captured by a great love, he will find himself going places and doing things that he himself would never have considered. If tradition is right and Peter did ask to be crucified head down (because he felt unworthy to be crucified like his Lord), then truly a great love had captured him, for he did what the old Simon would never have done.

Love is the source of real courage. Few people are born fearless, and those who are truly fearless do not live long. But when a man loves something more than he fears the opposition or consequences that may come with that love, then he has courage. This kind of courage is available, even to those of us who are most fearful.

We all need and want love. But we fear great love! Love as great as the love God has extended to us in Christ will woo from us the sovereignty of our own life. If we respond to His great love, one day He will bring us to the place where we realize we are not our own and that we are no longer calling the shots. At that point, we shall know what freedom and life are all about, because we shall experience both.

The obvious question to ask at this point is, "How can I have this kind of love?" Jesus gives us the simple—but not easy—answer in the sermon on the mount.

> Keep on asking, and the gift will be given you; keep on seeking, and you will find; keep on knocking, and the door will open to you. For everyone who keeps on asking, receives, and everyone who keeps on seeking, finds, and to the one who keeps on knocking, the door will open. What human father among you, when his son asks him for bread, will give him a stone? Or if he asks for a fish, will he give him a snake? So if you, in spite of your being bad, know how to give your children what is good, how much more surely will your heavenly Father give what is good to those who keep on asking Him?[6]

He gives good gifts. If I ask for a million dollars He might say, "Son, you couldn't handle a million dollars; it would handle you and spoil you." It takes a mature person to manage great wealth and to keep it from mastering him. But if I ask for a love for Jesus Christ and His purpose that would be the burning passion of my life, then I suspect He would say, "Son, that will make you rich indeed, and I will give it to you."

To operate on that kind of fuel (without blowing up the engine) takes some doing. The Lord will have to take us a step at a time toward this intense love for Him. This brings us to a real hang-up. Most of us probably think that to be given this kind of love would mean being lifted to a higher echelon of spirituality where there would be no real problems or struggles. Nothing could be further from the truth. For Him to increase our capacity to love means that He will increase our capacity for bearing a greater part of the hurt, misery, and "lostness" of the people who live in our part of the jungle. This great love will push us out into a greater involvement in Christ's redemptive mission. It will cause us to pour out our lives for others!

One man said to me recently, "Quite frankly, I don't want that kind of love, if that is what it will cause me to do." He spoke the truth for all of us. We are desperately afraid of being loved with a great love and we are afraid of loving deeply. Yet there is nothing safer than that kind of love. Duty has boundaries and even going beyond one's duty still has limits. But love knows no extremity. It suffers long; it endures all things; and it bears all things. According to I Corinthians 13, all else may fail, but love never fails. There may be times when it seems as though it has failed. The cross of Christ no doubt looked like a failure on that fateful day. But as it turned out, it was a day of victory for God and man. And that victory was fully demonstrated in the Resurrection. Love never fails!

Once we realize how costly great love is, we will recognize in ourselves a resistance to it. This is a symptom of the disease called sin within each one of us. The best we can do, with God's help, is to pray, "Oh, Lord, I want to *want* to love You more deeply than I love my own life. Help me really to desire this." This is a real start! The next day, in the thick of life, He will begin to answer our prayer, and we will probably begin to complain. The next time we are inspired sufficiently to risk such request, we will add, "Lord, listen to me now, and not tomorrow when the going gets tough and I begin to balk. Give me a passionate love for You at all costs."

The person who dares to keep on asking will progressively experience God's love welling up inside, to be poured out for the sake of those about him. And the more he gives of this love, the more love he will receive.

I certainly have not been completely captured by this great love, but I have tasted it and the taste was good. I have also known the fear of punishment, and the hope of reward motivation. Because I once lived with this limiting attitude, I could never fully accept Paul's statement, "For I could wish that I myself were cursed and cut off from Christ for the sake of my brothers, those of my own race."[7] How could he be telling the truth? Could he have such concern and love for his own people that he would be willing to go to hell if it would benefit them? He did have this kind of love!

Some time ago when we were visiting my parents, I went by the graves of some significant people in my life. I stopped at my grandfather's grave, and, with gratitude, gave thanks for the relationship we had shared. I went to the grave of a five-year-old cousin, who had been close to me. His death still raises many questions in my mind. He was so full of life, and yet his life had been cut short by a rare blood disease. He was dead, and I was alive and healthy—and through no choice of our own. I must confess, this gave me an added sense of my stewardship of life. Life is a gift to be spent for the good of others. To grasp life selfishly is to lose it. But to give ourselves generously to God to be spent for others is to live life to the fullest.

I visited the grave of my first pastor. He was the man who had baptized me and had counseled and encouraged me over a period of several years. Again, I offered thanks to God for what He had given me through this godly man. Then I visited the grave of a girl with whom I had grown up. There was never anything romantic in our relationship, but she was as good a friend as I have ever had. We went to the state competition in extemporaneous speech together. After our high school days I saw her very seldom. Some years later, she committed suicide. This act was so contrary to the girl I knew that it was an emotional shock which left many questions in my mind—as well as some guilt. Had those of us who were close to her failed her in some way? Could I have extended our relationship beyond high school? My guilt was compounded by a feeling I had a few months before her death that I should go to see her. I never went. At her grave I gave thanks to God for what He had given me through her and asked for forgiveness for failing her. Her grave reminded me again of my own helpless humanity.

I made two other stops on the way back to my car. One

was at the grave of my wife's grandfather. I knew him before I knew my wife. He was a deacon at a church where I preached from time to time over a period of several years. This man had given me encouragement and had shown faith in me before I had much in myself. Again I gave thanks.

The last stop was unplanned. It was at the grave plot next to my wife's grandfather's grave. It belongs to us, and will, in all probability, be the place where my wife and I will be buried. It was a strange feeling to stand beside my own gravesite. It made me face some questions that I had otherwise avoided or taken lightly. Why am I alive? What does the future hold? What is it that really counts?

In the midst of these thoughts came a prayer from within. "Lord, all I ask is for You to let me live to make a truly significant contribution to at least one other human being for Your glory." Then I wept like a child. I felt that I was really free—free from the fear of punishment and the hope of reward; free to live and to love, and trust the rest to God.

I dare you, as I dare myself, to ask God to give us a love for Him, for His purpose in history and beyond, that runs deeper than the love of our own life. Dare to taste a greatness that this world knows nothing about.

BEYOND THIS GOD CANNOT GO

Behold! A world! And worlds!
Light. And dark.
Sun. And Moon.
From Where?

Before time. Before light.
Before anything, was God.
"In the beginning God."
God created!

"And God said," . . . and it was so.
Firmament. Dry land. Heaven and earth.
Waters together. Seas.
"And it was good."

A world, yes. But more. Life!
Grass, herb, trees—seed to bear.
Fishes, fowl, beast; the tiny, creeping thing.
This, too, was good.

Before—nothing. Now—so much.
Galaxy beyond galaxy. Time.
Living things. But all "things."
No "one."

Again, God labored.
In the mist, He knelt.
In the dust, He toiled.
In His own image, He created.

Ah! A new creature.
More precious than all before.
God cradled this creature.
Into it, He breathed His life.

A living soul! Some "one."
A person. Man!
Man to share His creation!
Could God do more?

Creation. Man. God.
Perfect fellowship.
Until . . .

Sin. Broken fellowship. Separation.
How to bridge the gulf?
How to offer His life anew?
How to let man know?

Christ! His own Son! The God-Man!
First-born of a new race.
Man—in Christ—*now sons!*
Children. Heirs.

Sons, to share His very Life. And,
Beyond this God cannot go!

VERDELL DAVIS

EPILOGUE

"They have found the plane. It's a positive identification. It is at about 10,000 feet and it's broken up pretty bad. There's no sign of anyone around. We're waiting on a helicopter that can fly up that high, and we'll call you back. But . . . it doesn't look good."

Ann Clark, Lucy Mabery, Gail Schoellkopf and I were sitting in the dining room around a speaker phone when we heard those words. Our husbands were on that plane. Soon we received the final message—"There are no survivors." In a moment, in the twinkling of an eye, in an unexplained airplane crash in the mountains of Cody, Wyoming, they were ushered into the presence of the Lord they loved and served. We walked from that room into the warm embraces of hundreds of friends who had been crying, laughing, hoping and praying through the long vigil with us. They loved our husbands, too: George Clark, chairman of the board and chief executive officer of MBank, Dallas; Dr. Trevor E. Mabery, ear, nose and throat surgeon; Hugo W. Schoellkopf III, sporting goods manufacturer; and the Reverend Creath Davis, minister and executive director of Christian Concern Foundation.

The vigil began for us on Sunday afternoon, June 28, 1987. The night before we each had talked with our husbands. They had been excited about the fellowship and sharing they had enjoyed at the Focus on the Family men's retreat there at Elk Canyon Ranch, but they were ready to get home to their own families. Their Cessna 421 lifted off the runway in White Sulpher Springs, Montana, early that Sunday morning in order to be home in Dallas before 2:00 P.M. The afternoon wore on very slowly when they were not home on time. By early evening we were at Gail Schoellkopf's taking the first steps of alerting the authorities and trying to decide who of friends and family to contact— and what to tell them, because we knew nothing. Soon the house was filling with concerned friends and before midnight the first of hundreds of people to become involved in a three-day air search left Dallas on the MBank plane. Many of us spent the night together at Gail's, whose home became the communication and gathering center.

As word spread, planes, men, and our own sons left Dallas to join the Civil Air Patrol of both Montana and Wyoming in the search. Lynch Flying Service turned over their entire facilities located at the Billings, Montana, airport to be the control center for the more than 25 private aircraft flying missions over several thousand square miles of mountains. Eventually the Air Force lent some of their more sophisticated equipment for a period of twenty-four hours. As the search progressed more than 300 people had become involved in some significant way, leaving their businesses and giving of their time and resources to serve as pilots, spotters, ground crew, maintenance technicians, communications coordinators, and organizers. And everywhere it was evident—people cared enough to do what needed to be done to find one small plane carrying four very loved and respected men.

In Dallas, the caring for the families of the four men was no less evident. We were surrounded by loving friends and our every need was met by someone standing by. The community was stunned by the prospect of losing four of its own, and thousands across the nation followed the unfolding of the search and the coming together of a city to watch and pray. The news media were sensitive to our privacy but very vocal about the men. Almost every newscast carried some reference to the Christian faith of these men. There was no way to miss the message that whatever these men did vocationally, their primary commitment was to the Lord and their families.

The plane was found on Wednesday, July 1, in the Absorka Mountains of northwestern Wyoming. The sons were flown from Billings to Cody because they wanted to be the ones to identify their dads. Those young men had matured in this intense life experience and as they talked together they asked themselves, "Is that the last memory we want of our dads?" They agreed, no. Instead their final mission of these long three days was to fly over the crash site and pray that the Lord would give them the kind of commitment for Him and His purpose that their fathers had. Then they said, "Let's go home."

Our four families had been involved with each other for many years in Christian ministries, hunting and fishing trips, family dinners, and had laughed, cried and prayed together enough to feel very much a part of each other's lives. Now that friendship and oneness of spirit, and the deeper bonding that had occurred over the days of waiting, allowed us to give strength to each other for moving together through the stresses of the next few days.

July 3 found us first at the graveside with Gail as by words and action Hugo's body was committed to the grave. Later we stood with Lucy at Trevor's grave. And after that with Ann as George was buried.

At 5:00 P.M. we walked into Park Cities Baptist Church with our families and 3500 friends. We heard Jenni Rasberry's clear voice singing,

When peace like a river attendeth my way,
When sorrows like sea billows roll;
Whatever my lot, Thou hast taught me to say,
"It is well, it is well with my soul."

We listened to our ministers from Park Cities Baptist Church, Highland Park Presbyterian Church, and Northwest Bible Church talk about our husbands and the Lord they loved. They asked the questions with us: "Why? Why these four men? Why now?" And they left the answers with our loving, sovereign God whose "ways are not our ways" but who is infinitely good and wise.

We cried quietly as we heard Dr. James Dobson say to our children:

> I want to tell you something—and you already know this. You had great men for fathers. Great men. Not because of what they accomplished, and they did accomplish a lot, but because of the way they lived their lives, because of the way they loved,

because of the way they gave, because of the way they served. They were great men. And if they were here today in the flesh to give you a message, I believe at the top of the list they would say, "Remain faithful to the cause of Christ. Above all else, hold on to your faith. Do not give Satan a place for mischief in your life."

Keep the circle unbroken, for your fathers are not buried. Your fathers are alive. All four of them are alive, and we will be reunited with them someday. I know that they are there.

They love you. They had talked at length with me about it. They loved their families more than anything in this world.

Dr. Clayton Bell concluded the service:

> Dear People. We are gathered here out of respect for the memory of George Clark, Creath Davis, Trevor Mabery, and Hugo Schoellkopf. Our community, our churches, our nation, and our world need a whole army of obedient soldiers of Jesus Christ who will live their lives by putting the Lord and their families first and letting all of our other commitments and involvements flow out of our relationship of obedience to our Lord. Will you be one of them?
>
> I want us to take just a few moments of silence and let you quietly, in your own heart, respond to God as He prompts you. And if you are willing at this point to say, "Yes, I want to take the place of one of these four men," won't you tell God in the quietness of this moment and in the silence of your own heart.

As people stood visiting outside the church on that hot rainless July day, a rainbow was clearly visible in a wisp of clouds just over the church steeple. A photograph taken during the service shows a small plane cradled in the upturned rainbow—truly God's promise to us that our husbands are in the glorious presence of the Lord, and the Lord will walk with us through each step of this painful journey.

But there was one more day in this long week. On Saturday, July 4, was the funeral service and burial for Creath in the small central Texas town where he and I both grew up. I would never have asked the other families and so many friends to make that trip after all they had been through. But they came, and what a blessing and a comfort to have them there. How fitting to close this chapter of our lives by lifting our voices together in the Psalm Creath himself had read at many a graveside—"The Lord is my shepherd, I shall not want . . ."

VERDELL DAVIS

CREATH DAVIS

A man of strength, clothed in gentleness, spontaneity and understanding, with a single focus to his life. He helped us to capture the vision of our greatness in God's sight. That mission never wavered, a mission to make us thirsty to join him on a mutual pilgrimage with Jesus Christ, that we might grasp our Father's love and acceptance and forgiveness.

As our earthly model, he left an indelible mark of authenticity and transparency. He was the same on the inside as on the outside, with little pretense.

He came to grow a family from all walks—to mold us together. And from our diversity came a unity, an indivisible bond to support and undergird.

He came to lead our fellowship for one purpose—to bring out the best in us, to believe in us, to equip us to be a team of champions, that we might reach out beyond ourselves.

He came to love us—to celebrate our joys and to grieve our sorrows, to help us gain a perspective that nothing is wasted in God's economy, that all our experiences, whether bitter or sweet, will somehow, some way be woven together to glorify our Heavenly Father.

He came to be our friend—wearing a mantle of acceptance, giving us the freedom to reveal our inward parts. And with kindness, he blew the chaff away.

He came to be God's friend—laying down his life while a sojourner on this earth to teach and serve and love his Father's children.

He made a difference beyond measure with his single focus, by what he believed and how he lived what he believed. Our response is one of profound gratitude that God gave us the desire of our heart in walking a few steps together.

Now he has made his grand entrance to the other side. Until we follow him, shall we join hands together and make a difference also.

Well done, Creath. Our cup runneth over.

MARTHA FRENCH

ACKNOWLEDGMENTS

Grateful acknowledgment is made to the following for permission to use copyright material:

The Westminster Press
> From *The Strong and the Weak* by Paul Tournier, published in Switzerland in 1948. First published in English by SCM Press, Ltd. in 1963.

Roger Lincoln Shinn
> From *Christianity and the Problem of History*, published by The Bethany Press, copyright ©1953 by Roger L. Shinn.

Baker Book House
> From *A Christian Approach to Philosophy* by Warren C. Young, copyright ©1954.

Harper and Row, Publishers, Inc.
> From *The Healing Partnership* by Bernard Steinzor, copyright ©1967.

Charles Scribner's Sons
> From *I and Thou* by Martin Buber, copyright ©1958.

The Seabury Press
> From *The Creative Years* by Reuel Howe, copyright © 1959 by The Seabury Press, Inc.

World Publishing, Times Mirror
> From an essay by David Maitland published in *A Handbook of Christian Theology*, Marvin Halverson and Arthur A. Cohen, Editors, copyright ©1958 by The World Publishing Company.

Fleming H. Revell Company
> From *The New Immorality* by David A. Redding. Copyright ©1967 by Fleming H. Revell Company, Old Tappen, N.J.

From *God's Psychiatry* by Charles L. Allen, Copyright © 1953 by Fleming H. Revell Company, Old Tappan, N.J.

Zondervan Publishing House
> From *The Art of Understanding Yourself* by Cecil G. Osborne, copyright ©1967.
> From *Practical Christian Ethics* by C.B. Eavey, copyright ©1959.

John Knox Press
  From *To Understand Each Other* by Paul Tournier, copyright ©1962.
Van Nostrand Reinhold Company
  From *The Transparent Self* by Sidney Jourard, copyright ©1964 by Litton Educational Publishing, Inc.; by permission of Van Nostrand Reinhold Company
Prentice-Hall, Inc.
  From *Psycho-Cybernetics* by Maxwell Maltz, copyright ©1960 by Prentice-Hall, Inc.
Scripture used is from *King James Version* unless otherwise stated.
  Other translations used are *The New International Version, Good News for Modern Man*, and Charles B. Williams translation, and the J.B. Phillips translation.

My wife, Verdell, and good friend, Gwen Pollock did a real labor of love in helping to edit this manuscript, along with Dawson and Martha French. The late Nat Tracy, friend and teacher for twenty years, contributed enormously to the content of this book. Other professors who have helped me and encouraged me in this venture are John Newport, John Drakeford, William L. Hendricks, Jack Gray, Cal Guy, Huber Drumwright, Robert Coleman, John Kiwiet, Milton Ferguson, C.W. Scudder, Jesse Northcutt and Roy Fish, all of whom are or were on the faculty of Southwestern Baptist Theological Seminary.

My thanks to the two churches I served as pastor during the time much of the content for this book was taking shape.

A word of thanks is in order to the people who have been a part of the Christian Concern Foundation fellowship through the years. This community has nurtured us and enabled us to explore God's call in a very unique arena. The people who have participated in our retreats at Kaleo Lodge, in our Bible studies, sharing groups, therapy groups and conferences of various kinds have kept this writing endeavor from being purely academic.

142 / ACKNOWLEDGMENTS

I wish also to say thanks to the Christian Concern Foundation Board of Directors for their support and encouragement in every respect: Jodie and Dottie Thompson, George and Miley Busiek, George and Ann Clark, Roy and Janis Coffee, Charles and Gwen Davis, Jack and Fran Davis, Don and Mary Ann Edney, Larry and Fran Honea, Dan and Jimmie Abbott, Dan and Martha Lou Beaird, Tommy and Patricia Jones, Ray and Sharon Powell, Hugo and Gail Schoellkopf; *and others of the fellowship:* John and Sybil Allison, David and Nancy Burgher, Allen Campbell, Ron and Barbara Grusendorf, Charley and Aggie Johnson, Charlie and Myrna Little, Dick and Charlotte Miller, Leland and Nona Bell Long, Louis and Fay Beth Moore, John and Frances Saville, Al and Sue Simmons, Lee and Joanie Slaughter, Fred and Louise Smitham, Robert and Sally Stout, Jim and Susie Tubb, Bob and Betty Williams, Tex and Lavana Williams, Bruce and Rusty Wilson, Jack and Nance Wilson, Julian and Ann Rorie, Jim and Sherri Hutchinson, Mike Godwin, John and Patsy Jones, Parker and Lois Folse, Tommy and Scottie Miller, Jack and Florence Reed, Bill and Peggy Simpkin, Robert and Eve Williams, Bill and Mary Lou Chesnut, Larry Fleck, Dean and Patsy Coppage, Martin and Karen Cude, Roy and Lindy Downey, Jerry and Carole Duval, Joe and Carol Simpson, David and Ann Carruth, Russell and Lisa Johnson, Jim and Pam Graham, Lonnie and Lorry Holotik, Jim and Terry Wilson; *and others involved:* Arthur and Cookie Woods, Dr. and Mrs. Donovan Campbell, Gordon and Patsy Campbell, Mike and Mary Ann Denton, Wallace and Mary Margaret Finfrock, Doug and Mary Ellen Forde, Greg and Betsy Gallagher, John and Kathy Jackson, Phyllis Ann Jones, John and Sandra Kidd, Gladys Lankford, Frank and Markay Marshall, Kay Schaefer, David and Litty Turner, Mrs. J.B. Woods, and Clyde and Betsy Jackson.

Finally, a word of thanks to Carmen Conner and the Heights Baptist Church of Albuquerque, New Mexico for allowing me to present this book in lecture form before it was published, and to Vicki Hesterman for her editorial help.

NOTES

CHAPTER 1   HOW TO BEGIN THE JOURNEY WITH GOD

[1] In the Hebrew manuscript the word "God" is used rather than the word "angels" (which is given in the Greek Septuagint).
[2] Genesis 1:27.
[3] II Corinthians 5:19.
[4] Revelation 22:17.
[5] John 5:39, *Good News for Modern Man.*
[6] Matthew 9:12.

CHAPTER 2   KEEPING UP THE APPEARANCES

[1] Paraphrase of Galatians 2:11 and 14.
[2] II Corinthians 12:9-10, *Good News for Modern Man.*
[3] Ephesians 4:15.
[4] See Ephesians 4:15.
[5] See I Corinthians 8:13. Paraphrased.
[6] From *The Strong and the Weak* (pp. 20-21) by Paul Tournier, translated by Edwin Hudson. Published in the United States by The Westminster Press, 1963. Used by permission.

CHAPTER 3   WHAT ABOUT MY PAST?

[1] John 5:6, *Good News for Modern Man*
[2] Cecil G. Osborne, *The Art of Understanding Yourself,* Grand Rapids: Zondervan Publishing House, 1967), p. 11.
[3] John 1:9.
[4] Psalm 32:3-4.
[5] II Samuel 12:7.
[6] Psalm 32:1-2.

CHAPTER 4 WHAT ABOUT MY FUTURE?
[1] Colossians 1:15-17, *Phillips.*
[2] Matthew 28: 18:20.
[3] Romans 8:31b.
[4] Philippians 4:6-7, 12-13, *Good News for Modern Man.*

CHAPTER 5 THE NEED FOR SELF-ACCEPTANCE
[1] Matthew 22:37-39.
[2] Matthew 16:24-25.
[3] Romans 6:6
[4] Galatians 2:20.
[5] Matthew 16:26, *Good News for Modern Man.*
[6] Proverbs 23:7a.
[7] Maxwell Maltz, *Psycho-Cybernetics,* (New York: Essandess Special Editions, 1960), p. viii.
[8] John 8:58.
[9] Exodus 3:14.
[10] Luke 22:24.
[11] John 13:3-5, *New International Version (NIV).*
[12] Philippians 4:9, *NIV.*
[13] Romans 8:29.
[14] Ephesians 2:7, *NIV.*
[15] John 3:2b, *NIV*
[16] I John 4:10-13, 20-21, *NIV*

CHAPTER 6 GOD'S MAGNIFICENT OBSESSION
[1] Roger Lincoln Shinn, *Christianity and the Problem of History,* (St. Louis: The Bethany Press, 1953), p. 16.
[2] Proverbs 29:18.
[3] Warren C. Young, *A Christian Approach to Philosophy* (Grand Rapids, Michigan: Baker Book House, 1954), p. 81.
[4] Philippians 2:11.
[5] Ephesians 1:7-12, *Phillips.*
[6] II Peter 1:4, *Phillips.*
[7] Revelation 3:20.
[8] Matthew 5:13a, 14a.

[9] John 17:15-16, 18, *NIV*
[10] Ephesians 1:18b, *Williams*
[11] I Peter 1:12c.
[12] Ephesians 2:7.
[13] I Corinthians 2:9, *NIV*

CHAPTER 7 ISOLATION IS INSANITY

[1] Bernard Steinzor, *The Healing Partnership*, (New York: Harper and Row, 1967), p. 245.
[2] *Ibid.*, p. 245.
[3] Genesis 2:18, 21-24, *NIV*.
[4] Martin Buber, *I and Thou*, (New York: Charles Scribner's Sons, 1958), p. 11.
[5] Steinzor, *Op. cit.*, p. 244.
[6] Sidney Jourard, *The Transparent Self*, Princeton, N.J.:D. Van Nostrand Co., 1964), p.26 (Insight Book Edition).
[7] Buber, *Op. cit.*
[8] *Ibid.*
[9] John 17:2-3, *NIV.*
[10] John 10:10.
[11] Colossians 2:9, *NIV.*
[12] Hebrews 1:1-2, 3a, *NIV.*
[13] I John 3:1-2, *NIV.*
[14] Matthew 16:16b.
[15] John 21:25.
[16] John 21:25, *NIV.*
[17] John 1:14b, *NIV.*
[18] Ephesians 2:10a, *NIV.*
[19] Ephesians 2:8-9, *NIV.*
[20] Romans 8:32, *NIV.*
[21] II Corinthians 5:17-19, *NIV.*
[22] I Peter 1:12, *NIV.*
[23] John 15:4-5.

CHAPTER 8 FOR BETTER OR FOR WORSE

[1] Paul Tournier, *To Understand Each Other*, (Richmond, Virginia: John Knox Press, 1962), pp. 12-13.
[2] Genesis 2:18, *NIV.*

[3]Genesis 2:24, *NIV.*
[4]Tournier, *To Understand Each Other,* p. 13.
[5]Exodus 20:14.
[6]Ephesians 5:23,25.
[7]Ephesians 5:22.

CHAPTER 9   WHAT ABOUT MY VOCATION?
[1]Luke 9:23, *Williams.*
[2]John 14:18a.
[3]Genesis 2:2.
[4]Genesis 1:28, 2:15, *NIV.*
[5]John 4:34, *NIV.*
[6]II Corinthians 5:17, *Williams.*
[7]Ephesians 6:5-9, *Williams.*
[8]Reuel Howe, *The Creative Years,* (New York: The Seabury Press, 1959), p. 182.
[9]Marvin Halverson and Arthur A. Cohen, Editors, *A Handbook of Christian Theology,* (New York: The World Publishing Company, 1958), Essay by David Maitland, p. 372.
[10]Ephesians 4:1.
[11]Exodus 20:9-10a.
[12]David A. Redding, *The New Immorality,* (New Jersey: Fleming H. Revell Company, 1967), pp. 72-73.
[13]Charles L. Allen, *God's Psychiatry,* (New Jersey: Fleming H. Revell Company, 1953), p. 58.
[14]Psalm 46:10a.
[15]Luke 12:15, *Williams.*
[16]C.B. Eavey, *Practical Christian Ethics,* (Michigan: Zondervan Publishing House, 1959), p. 179.
[17]Psalm 24:1, *NIV.*
[18]Exodus 20:15.

CHAPTER 10   NOT FOR MY SAKE ALONE
[1]John 15:16, *Williams.*
[2]Acts 9:15-16, *NIV.*
[3]Philippians 3:3-14, *Williams.*
[4]Matthew 23:11, *NIV.*

[5]John 1:3, 10, *NIV.*
[6]Colossians 1:16-17, *NIV.*
[7]Job 1; Hebrews 2:14-15; I John 3:8.
[8]John 13:12-16, *Williams*
[9]Philippians 2:13, *Williams*
[10]Matthew 25:40.
[11]Ephesians 2:10, *NIV.*
[12]John 15:15, *Williams.*

CHAPTER 11   FINDING AN ADEQUATE MOTIVATION FOR THE JOURNEY

[1]Genesis 22:16-18, *NIV.*
[2]John 13:38, Paraphrased.
[3]Luke 22:61-62, *NIV.*
[4]John 21:16, *NIV.*
[5]John 21:18-19, *NIV.*
[6]Matthew 7:7-11, *Williams.*
[7]Romans 9:3, *NIV.*